"In the era of school shootings and campus sexual assaults, this book couldn't be more timely."

Doug Lynch, Public Safety Trainer

This book delivers a plan for transforming your approach to personal safety

Do you know the skills you need to keep yourself safe? This book will change the way you approach your world and help keep you safer in it!

In *Confidence In Conflict For Campus Life,* you'll learn:

- How to assess a new campus for vulnerabilities and risk indicators

- "When-Then Thinking" and "540° Proxemic Management"

- A practical approach to threat assessment

- How to navigate awkward situations and conflicts with friends

- Verbal defense and how to communicate under stress

- Realistic and effective bystander intervention strategies

- How to address hazing and sexual assault

- What to do in the event of a school shooting or mass casualty incident

These strategies are taught through Vistelar, a global consulting and training institute focused on addressing the spectrum of human conflict at the point of impact — from before an interaction begins through to the consequences of how an interaction is managed.

Vistelar's clients come from fields such as law enforcement, health care, loss prevention, security, education, customer service and business.

Hear From Our Readers

"Never have I seen as timely a book that prepares our children to stay safe away from home. I wish I had a copy when I went away to school, but at least I can give a copy to my grandchildren as they go to college."

— Bob "Coach" Lindsey, Law Enforcement Trainer

"At a time in history when violence prevention is getting more needed attention, Jill's book gives readers of all ages and genders the knowledge and skills to make college environments safer for themselves and those around them. It's a great read that fills a void in the world of violence prevention!"

— Chris Daood, Sexual Violence Prevention Educator

"The content of the book outlines solid, fundamental skills needed in today's society. Jill does a good job referencing her own experiences, other experts, and research when explaining points. This would be a fine read for students entering campus life, taking a conflict management course, or even an oral-interpersonal communications course."

— Jessica Brogley, College Professor

"This book is perfect for not only the college student but for anyone. It's very informative and gives you perspective on situations and experiences you might not think of. It's a good read and provides scenarios to bring you in and keep you interested. Great book!"

— Amanda LaFaive, Former College Student & Young Professional

---

"College students and parents sending their kids to college NEED TO READ THIS and apply the things shared! Great book, educates, inspires, shares new ideas on personal safety for campus life."

— Dave Young, Defensive Tactics Instructor

"As students head to campus, whether as incoming freshmen or returning upperclassmen, there's much on their minds — meeting friends, settling in and starting classes. Assault, danger and theft are most likely not among their concerns. That lack of awareness poses a problem for the students and for the campus community in which they live. No one knows that fact better than Jill Weisensel, a campus law enforcement Lieutenant and national crisis communications trainer. Weisensel has seen the sad underside of campus life, when things can go badly.

By having guided countless students through the aftermath of a safety breach, she has the wisdom and the perspective to help others ... before bad things happen to good people. I read this book not only from the vantage point of a Vistelar author myself, but also as the mother of teen-agers who will be packing up and heading for college in two short years. I'd recommend it for students, parents and faculty/staff alike. This book is relevant, full of real-life examples that happen on college campuses across the country. It's also easy to understand how a safety mindset can help students (and everyone else on campus) become not just smarter — but wiser, too."

- Kathy Mangold, Author of *Confidence in Conflict for Everyday Life*

"This is a wonderful book! I understand that it is geared toward the college freshman, but anyone one can learn from this book. There are many examples that are applicable across the board. For instance, as a society, we've become so consumed by our phones, that we fail to be aware of our surroundings. Our heads buried in the screen, yet failing to notice what is happening around us- that should be sending out caution. The author points out things to look for, as well as gives you tools to deal with situations once you are in them. It's a must read for both students heading away from home for the first time, as well as parents! Very well written advice for the multitude of new, uncomfortable, awkward, and just plain illegal situations a naive, trusting person may encounter."

- Sue Palubicki, Professional First Responder

"Jill does a great job of detailing how to effectively handle the difficult situations that surround campus life. Through her vast experience, she is able to engage the reader while constantly providing valuable tips and information. This book is a must for any student that enjoys campus life."

- Bill Singleton, Police Officer

Confidence
IN / CONFLICT
FOR CAMPUS LIFE

The must-have safety resource
for every college bound student.

Jill Weisensel, M.S.

Truths Publishing
Milwaukee, WI

www.ConfidenceInConflict.com

For bulk-purchasing pricing, please contact:
  Vistelar
  1845 N. Farwell Ave., Suite 210
  Milwaukee, WI 53202
  Phone: 877-690-8230
  Fax: 866-406-2374
  Email: info@vistelar.com
  Web: www.vistelar.com

Weisensel, Jill
Confidence In Conflict For Campus Life / Jill Weisensel
Edited by Allen Oelschlaeger
Revised Edition 2017

ISBN 13: 978-0-9792734-8-3
ISBN 10: 0-9792734-8-X

LCCN: 2014952584

BISAC Subject Headings:
    EDUCATION / Violence & Harassment
    EDUCATION / Student Life & Student Affairs
    SELF-HELP / Communications & Social Skills

Published By Truths Publishing, Milwaukee, WI
Printed In the United States of America

Table of Contents

Introduction

For many of you, the college experience will be your first time away from home and away from your friends and family. You will find yourself in an unfamiliar environment, and in a position to do what you want, when you want, and how you want. While the college campus environment sets the stage for some of the most fun and exciting experiences of your lives, it is also one that poses many risks.

During the first few weeks of school, you will find yourself the most vulnerable to all sorts of situations that you may have never experienced before. You must learn how to navigate campus (possibly even a new city), meet new people and determine who you can trust, and tackle a much different academic class load. You will experience competing interests for your time between friends, studying, sports, and parties, and your decision-making skills will be put to the test like never before.

In working in campus security and law enforcement for the past decade, I witness this "freshman" experience every year. I have the privilege to witness some of the fun and happy times, like move-in, the first day of school, big sporting events against rival teams, and graduation. Unfortunately, I also have to live through the negative experiences: the ones that no one likes to talk about, no one likes to think about, and no one wants to admit could happen during their time away at school.

The reality is this: bad things will, and do happen, on college campuses all over the country. Textbooks, backpacks, bikes, and laptops get stolen. Wallets, purses, and cash disappear. Apartments and dorm rooms get burglarized. People get robbed, and there are school shootings. While many students abstain from drinking alcohol, many others don't. Of those that do, many drink responsibly, while others consistently drink a lot. It's not my goal to moralize, but as a public safety professional I see the impact of these actions firsthand. Excessive alcohol consumption contributes to a daunting list of problems on campus, including medical incidents from acute intoxication, medical incidents as a result of falls, hazing, bar fights, car accidents, the destruction of property, dating violence, and sexual assault—problems that numerous campus officials work very, very hard to combat every year. The National Institute on Alcohol Abuse and Alcoholism indicates that an estimated 1,825 college students (between the ages of 18-24) die every year from alcohol related unintentional injuries, including motor vehicle crashes. This is in addition to an estimated 599,000 students (between the ages of 18-24) who are unintentionally injured under the influence of alcohol *every year*.

The costs of these incidents go far and beyond the incidents themselves, as many of these behaviors have both school misconduct and legal ramifications. A drunken bar fight could lead to both a disorderly conduct ticket and a school suspension. Throwing up excessively and passing out from alcohol intoxication will most likely result in a very expensive trip to the hospital, including the cost of an ambulance (upwards of $2,000) and an emergency room bill. And when you're dealing with the real-life consequences of hazing and sexual assault, the dollar cost is nothing compared to the lifelong social and psychological repercussions of these incidents.

While it's easy to look at these things and think, "That could never happen to me," the reality is that yes, it could. The victim of a tragedy and the victim of a crime have one thought in common: "I never thought it could happen to me."

I have presented my work at various national conferences, including several of the Vistelar National Conferences, and the National Association of Student Personnel Administrators in Higher Education Regional and National Conferences, and the International Association of Campus Law Enforcement Administrators Conferences. As a campus security professional who has researched over 30 years of campus safety programs and violence prevention initiatives, I am often asked, "What would you want your child to know before they left for college?" After several years of crime prevention experience and law enforcement training, it is my goal with this book to provide the college bound student with the absolute best "must-have" safety information, before they get to school. While the collaborative work of campus officials and orientation staff members is unwavering and critically important, I also know that their message is often too late. Students need this information and need to learn these personal safety and conflict management skills before they arrive on campus, which is ultimately their new home for the next four (or more) years.

The skills you will learn throughout this book are life skills. They are skills that you will definitely want to have and not need, rather than not have, and need them during a time of crisis.

Throughout the course of this book, you will learn:

- How to improve your personal safety and increase awareness of your surroundings.

- How to identify red flags of high risk behaviors and identify risk indicators of potential threats.

- How to reduce those risk factors in real scenarios.

- How to communicate under pressure and in potentially hostile situations.

- How to identify, reduce, and react to risk.

- How and when to safely intervene when you witness something going wrong.

Chapter 1
Your First Class - Personal Situational Awareness 101

After an awesome summer break filled with concerts and days at the beach, it was finally Amanda's college move-in day. As her parents pulled up in front of her dorm, she was surprised at just how many people were running around like crazy trying to unload books, food, clothes, and futons. Everybody seemed to have so much "new stuff." There were new flat screen TVs and mini-fridges, and boxes and boxes of new laptops. She was amazed when she looked up and saw a pile of someone's stuff left unattended. "Look mom, that's a brand new Macbook Pro. That's got to be like $1,800! I can't believe someone would just walk away from it like that." Amanda's mom looked back at her and smiled. "Don't worry honey; I'm sure there's hardly any crime here."

The belief that there's "no crime" on a college campus is just as misguided as the belief that bad things won't happen to good people. In fact, statistics show that over 500,000 college students become the victims of various crimes every year. We also know that bad things, unfortunate things, and accidents can happen to anyone at any time. But that doesn't mean you have to just sit around and wait for something bad to happen. Those of us in law enforcement receive a substantial amount of training pertaining to personal awareness, proxemic management, and threat assessment, so that we can put ourselves in the best position possible and make the safest decisions possible, without getting hurt while trying to help people. Most people I know that work in law enforcement have one wish for people who have no law enforcement experience: *they want you to think more like a cop.*

So what does that mean exactly? It means that you need to shift your thinking about what makes an environment safe, and you need training on how to see and evaluate your space in a new way. It means taking a different perspective about what could be a potential threat. It also requires people to shift their mindset from "It will never happen to me," to "I'm going to do everything possible to reduce my risk of that happening to me." Finally, it also means knowing that when bad things do happen, you will be prepared and capable of handling them in a way that lessens the likelihood of harm to you and others.

Now I'm not suggesting you become paranoid in thinking that everything and everyone poses a potential threat to you and your friends, but I am encouraging you to take ownership of your personal safety. I'm encouraging you to learn the skills you need to be mindful, not fearful.

So that brings me to my first question: *Who's responsible for maintaining your personal safety?*

Is it your parents? Is it your roommate? Did you say the police or campus security? If you answered yes to any one of those questions, you'd be wrong. The number one person responsible for maintaining your personal safety is—you! You are responsible for your own space and your emotional and physical well-being within it. You also play a part in creating an environment that promotes a safe and healthy environment for everyone to learn and live.

Over the course of the next several chapters I will present to you the skills you need to know in order to take your personal safety into your own hands, so that you will have a pre-planned and practiced response available to you when you need it the most. And while no one skill or set of strategies is guaranteed to keep you safe 100% of the time, you can rest assured knowing that if you learn these skills and are mindful of these strategies, you will be much less likely to become the victim of a crime. In other words, you will be better equipped to identify and avoid situations whereas you may be more vulnerable to crime. Regardless of what strategies you employ, you may still find yourself the victim of a crime. Please remember, it is not your fault. The only person who can truly prevent a crime from happening is the person committing it!

Second question: *If by some chance you would get into a situation that would require you to immediately react to save yourself or someone else, do you believe that you would do the right thing?*

If you answered yes to this question then you've probably found yourself in some type of dangerous situation like this before, or you've had self-defense or martial arts training. Some of you might have even said yes and thought, "Yeah, because my dad's a cop and he told me what to do." If you answered no, it's time to start learning the skills you need to keep yourself safe. Either way, read on. This book will help you understand what you need to do to respond appropriately.

It All Starts With When-Then Thinking

Even if you've never found yourself in a life threatening situation requiring split second decision making to save you or someone else, you can still prepare and "practice" for the worst by practicing "when-then thinking." The concept of when-then thinking was developed by nationally known and respected law enforcement trainer "Coach" Bob Lindsey. When-then thinking is the process of visualizing and thinking through what you would do in a given situation, even if it's

7

a situation that you've never been in before. In other words, when-then thinking is the skill of putting yourself into different types of scenarios so you can think through how you'd react to them *before* they happen. This is an important skill to have, because it isn't really a matter of *if* something bad will happen; it's a matter of *when*.

Young adults often experience something called "perceived invulnerability." Perceived invulnerability is the (false) belief that since nothing bad has ever happened to you; that nothing bad ever will. It is imperative to get past feeling "bulletproof," and recognize that there are in fact situations and different environmental variables that will make you more susceptible and vulnerable to crime. Otherwise, you will be caught by surprise when a bad situation does occur.

If you've never practiced when-then thinking, it can take a little getting used to, but the concept is actually quite simple. To practice, think of a situation in your life that has gone badly, or think of something bad that has happened to a friend. Then, imagine that it did happen, or that it was happening to you right now, and try to think about exactly how you would react.

My first experience with when-then thinking came at a young age. When I was five years old my mom dressed me up for a wedding. She curled my hair, put on my dress, and put me in some very flimsy bottom pink shoes with "cute" little bows on them. After my mom got dressed to leave, she came back into my room and noticed that I was sitting on my bed, very angry with my arms folded. I had also thrown the "cute" useless shoes across my room and onto the floor. My mom, extremely confused, asked me why I had thrown my shoes. I then, confidently as ever, walked across my room, picked up my favorite pair of Nike running shoes, and put them on. I said, "Mom. No. How would you expect me to run out of the building in case there was a fire?" From that moment on, my mom never, ever again asked me to wear impractical footwear.

Here's the point: At the wee age of five I was already becoming a tactical thinker. I was thinking about what could possibly happen while I was at the wedding. And while the possibility of a fire engulfing the church was slim to none, I still wanted to make sure I had the best chance of running out of there if my life depended on it. Again, when-then thinking is not meant to be catastrophic, and it's not meant to make you paranoid. It is meant to put you in the best and safest position possible so that you can appropriately respond in the case of an emergency. Notice I didn't say "react" in the case of an emergency. This is an important point. When you find yourself in a difficult situation (possibly even life threatening) you want to have a pre-planned, practiced, response in mind. If you have a plan, you will be able to respond appropriately, rather than react irrationally in a panic. Having pre-planned "actions" in mind will help you get through a frightening situation.

Maybe I Should Move That

Another drill for practicing when-then thinking is called, "Maybe I Should Move That." Don't laugh! It is actually quite eye-opening and effective. Many accidents and mishaps could be prevented if people would merely move something. That something could be an object, or that something could be yourself. We will talk more about "moving yourself" in Chapter Three. For now, I'd like you to think about how many cell phones you have seen broken. How many of those accidentally broken phones could have been prevented if they would have been moved away from the edge of the table? Or if the person texting on it would have moved themselves away from a door that was abruptly opened?

I had the opportunity to practice "Maybe I Should Move That" a short time ago, when I was loading my truck before driving to Illinois for a party. I didn't want to wear dress clothes all day, so I packed them in a bag, and set the bag on the back seat. Now remember, and this is important, that I only packed one outfit (a true when-then thinker would have packed a second set of clothes- just in case). I then loaded the snacks and appetizers that I was bringing to the party. As soon as I set the bag of snacks (which included a big jar of salsa and queso dip) on top of my bag of dress clothes, I thought to myself, "Oh man, maybe I should move that. That would be horrible if it spilled on my clothes while driving." So if you're ever struggling to think through how actions will play out (when-then thinking), try to think about what the result would be if something wouldn't have been moved.

"The most underutilized campus safety resource… is you!"

Chapter 2
Improving Your Personal Situational Awareness

After six hours of unloading her stuff and setting up her new dorm room, Amanda was exhausted. She was super excited that she finally had her own desk, her own bed, and her own space. She looked over at her laptop and iPod and noticed that her music download was finally complete. As she sat down on her futon, she heard a knock on her door. "That must be my roommate," she thought. Nervous to meet her, Amanda quickly opened the door. "Hi, I'm Jordan. I live here too."

Amanda looked at her new roommate in complete disbelief. Jordan was wearing dingy looking sports clothes, and smelled like she had just finished playing a lacrosse game. Jordan hardly had anything with her- just a backpack and a duffel bag. "Hi. Um... it's... nice...to meet you. I was just about to head to the cafeteria with some friends. If you leave later, could you please lock the door?" "Yeah, whatever. Later," said Jordan.

With Amanda gone, Jordan plunked down on her futon and debated whether or not she wanted to start setting up her stuff. "Nah," she thought. "I'm going to go check out this campus, it's huge." As Jordan left, she glanced over at Amanda's new laptop, noticed her iPod, and then scoped out all of her designer brand clothes. "Dang, the girl's got cash. She won't miss this." Jordan then took Amanda's iPod,

11

left their dorm room door unlocked, and headed out to scope the campus for some place to eat.

Theft happens just that fast. On a college campus theft is usually committed by the people you'd least expect to steal from you. In fact, over 80% of college crimes are "crimes of opportunity" committed by other members of the campus community and during broad daylight. A crime of opportunity simply means that the crime was committed because there was an opportunity for someone to get away with it. In other words, most of the time clothes, wallets, purses, bikes, cell phones, and laptops are stolen when they are left unsecured and unattended! Stealing something doesn't get any easier than someone leaving their property unattended, even if it's "just for a minute." I can't tell you how many police reports I have read that said, "The victim's unsecured and unattended property was stolen. The victim stated he walked away from his study table to go to the bathroom. When he returned to his table, his laptop was gone." As a rule of thumb, never leave anything unlocked or unattended that you can't afford to replace. Even more than that, think about the things that could get stolen that are irreplaceable, such as a gift from a parent or grandparent that has passed away, or a hard drive containing your final project. In terms of securing your personal property, it is always better to be safe than sorry. So what about Amanda's iPod? How could she have prevented it from being stolen?

First of all, Amanda poorly judged the situation. She left her property unattended with someone she had never met. She also trusted that person to lock up her room after she left. What if someone else came into their unlocked room after Jordan left? This is a very common way for TVs, DVDs, video game consoles, video games, and textbooks to get stolen. If Amanda had been utilizing when-then thinking, she would have thought about what she could do to prevent her iPod from being stolen, and about what she could do to make sure she got it back if it was stolen. The answer to the first question is easy: she shouldn't have left her iPod easily accessible and unattended with someone she didn't know. The answer to the second question is a little more difficult: she could have had her initials or a code word etched into the back of the iPod, so that if it was recovered by law enforcement personnel and found amongst Jordan's property, Amanda could prove it was hers.

Becoming a when-then thinker is just the first step to improving your personal situational awareness. The next step is to gain a better understanding of your "personal level of awareness," which is in essence your overall level of alertness. This also includes your overall understanding of the inherent dangers and resources available to you within your environment. Think of this like your own personal protection radar system.

Personal Levels of Awareness

To better explain this concept, I will reference world renowned tactical trainer Colonel Jeff Cooper's "Color Code," that has been used by law enforcement and military instructors for many years to describe "escalating degrees of preparedness" and alertness at any given time. While the Color Code model was originally intended for potentially combative and deadly force shooting incidents, public safety officials have universally adapted it to use as a gauge for all types of situations you may encounter.

The first condition of awareness is known as "Condition White." In Condition White, you are generally relaxed, and for the most part, unaware of what is going on around you and in your environment. Condition White is often referred to as a state of alertness equivalent to that of sleeping, meaning you're pretty much oblivious to everything happening around you. You are the most likely to become a victim of a crime if you're always living in Condition White.

Few of us intend to be in Condition White, but a lot of our behaviors can move us there. Being overtired, consuming drugs or alcohol, walking while texting, or walking with your headphones on— all of those things can impact your ability to "take in" information from your senses that can give you an accurate assessment as to how safe your environment is. Ideally, you should rarely, if ever, be in Condition White while on campus. If you were in Condition White and attacked, the attack would come as a total surprise to you, and you would not have any pre-planned response in mind. This would most likely result in complete panic.

The second condition of awareness is known as "Condition Yellow." In Condition Yellow, you remain relaxed, but you are now aware of who and what is around you. Think "relaxed, but alert." This simply means that you are now paying attention to all of the sights, smells, and sounds that surround you. It means that you have changed your level of alertness to recognize the actions of people around you, and you have started to casually think about how they could impact you and how you'd respond if something happened.

For example, if you were in Condition Yellow, you would start keeping track of people who were walking behind you and you would notice if they started following you when you turned a corner or entered a building. You would start to notice the sound of their footsteps quickening if they were trying to catch up to you, while also looking for a close public or private place that you could enter quickly so that you could get closer to people and away from danger. Some other examples of Condition Yellow thinking would include scanning for exits when entering a new building, or picking a seat in a theater or restaurant that would allow you to keep an eye on who may be entering the building. A great practical example of when-then thinking and Condition Yellow awareness would to be mindful of the time so that you can drive home safely on a Friday or Saturday night and get home before "bar close," which would increase the possibility of intoxicated drivers on the road.

The third condition of awareness is "Condition Orange." Condition Orange means that you have again escalated your level of alertness from just being "aware," to "being ready to act." In Condition Orange, you will have the ability to identify something of interest to you that may or may not prove to be a threat to you. Whatever that "something" is that you have identified as a possible threat, you will remain focused on it and will investigate it further to determine if it is a danger or not. If you identify someone or something that looks out of place or just doesn't "feel right," you should shift from 540 degree awareness, to a more focused awareness towards that danger, which will help you ascertain the true nature of the situation. In the example above, if you suddenly realized that you were being followed, you would start scanning for an area that had more light, more sound, and/or more people, and make a plan to head that way immediately. If you duck into a convenience store or head into a student common area, you can find safety amongst other students and see if the person following you was truly a threat. If they aren't, you have lost nothing, but at least you put yourself into a better position if in fact that person was a threat.

The fourth condition of awareness is "Condition Red." If you are scanning in Condition Orange and become aware of something that you have confirmed truly is a threat, you will move into Condition Red, which is also understood as the "action state." In this state, you will have specifically identified something you need to protect yourself against, and you will follow through with one of your mentally prepared when-then responses. In the example above, you would have already changed your course from walking home and would have made the decision to stop inside the convenience store, but you would also go a step further and perhaps let the store clerk know that you believe you're being followed and ask them to contact campus security.

There is a final condition of awareness that is referred to as "Condition Black." While not a part of Jeff Cooper's original model, I'm sure by now you can guess what level of alertness this is. Being the exact opposite of Condition White, Condition Black has often been referred to as the state of "blind panic." This would mean that something was happening to you or someone approached you that presented such a threat to your life that your body would immediately kick into a "fight or flight" response. This Condition would render you incapable of rational thought, and without proper training or sufficient experience, you would most likely "freeze," and be unable to respond to the situation. In our example above, if you were walking home at 2am, slightly intoxicated and looking down at your text messages (Condition White), and you were suddenly followed, grabbed, and were being robbed at gunpoint, your mind and body would most likely kick into a Condition Black panic.

One of the things to remember about the conditions of awareness is that they are fluid. You can move from one condition to another multiple times a day, or throughout a specific incident. It is possible to go right from Condition White to Condition Black (which is obviously not going to go well). It is also possible to be in Condition Yellow and hear something warranting concern, such as a woman screaming, moving you to Condition Orange or Condition Red, only to find out that the woman wasn't actually screaming out of fear, she was just shouting towards a friend who had forgotten something on the roof of his car and was driving away. This would move you back to Condition Yellow. This is just one example of how you can move through the conditions of awareness and use the Color Code strategy to evaluate your level of alertness. Try and think of situations and examples that you have already been in where this would have come in handy and perhaps helped the situation end differently.

Now that you have adopted the "scan and observe" mentality and understand the conditions of awareness, you will also need to learn how to trust your gut instincts. If something feels like it is out of place or you feel like you could be in danger, you need to trust your gut! Students often tell me that they don't know what dangerous cues to look for. We describe these cues as "red flags," which are basically risk indicators for things that make you more vulnerable to bad things happening, such as crimes, accidents, or medical emergencies. The better you are at identifying red flags, the better you will be at trusting your gut and avoiding potentially dangerous situations.

So What Exactly Is a Red Flag?

Red flag risk indicators vary depending on the environment. Think about the situations and places you will most likely find yourself in, and identify the warning signs. Any one warning sign doesn't necessarily mean you are in danger, but the totality of several may. Think about it like this: no one or two red flags should be considered in isolation, you should be assessing the totality of indicators to understand. Understand what they are, and what you can do to avoid or change them. We would like you to reduce your risk of being victimized—understanding red flag risk indicators and working to avoid them is a great risk reduction strategy! For example, here are some of the red flag risk indicators for a few common crimes on campus:

Bike Theft

A bicycle on campus is more likely to be stolen if:
- It is left unsecured in a bike rack or on a porch.
- It is secured with just a cable lock.
- It is secured with a cable lock, but only through the front tire.
- It is secured, but left unattended for long periods of time in a low lit, rarely traveled area.
- It isn't registered with the local police or campus security.

A bicycle on campus is less likely to be stolen if:
- It is properly secured with a "U-bolt" style lock.
- It is secured in a well-lit, well-traveled, well patrolled area.
- It is labeled or etched with a bike registration/recognition program with local police or campus security.

Burglary

An apartment on campus is more likely to be burglarized if:
- It is Spring Break or a holiday break and no one is around.
- It is located on a corner.
- It has multiple windows (entry points) on the first floor.
- The tenants continually leave the doors unlocked or open.
- The tenants leave boxes or packaging from high dollar items such

as laptops and TVs in the garbage out in front or back of the apartment/house.

- The tenants post on social media when they will be gone on vacation.

An apartment on campus is less likely to be burglarized if:

- The tenants keep the windows and doors on the first floor closed and locked.
- The tenants are mindful not to post on social media the days, times, and locations of their vacations.
- The tenants only host parties including friends they know well.
- The tenants do their best not to attract attention to their valuables by leaving boxes and packaging visible in their garbage.

Armed Robbery

An individual is more likely to be robbed if:

- They are walking in an unfamiliar place or in a high crime area.
- They are walking alone and/or in the dark.
- They aren't paying attention to their surroundings, such as by texting or listening to their headphones.
- They aren't paying attention to their surroundings as a result of being intoxicated or impaired by drugs.
- They have high dollar items, such as jewelry, purses, cell phones, or MP3 players externally visible.

An individual is less likely to be robbed if:

- They pay attention to their surroundings by walking to and from destinations with their headphones off and their cell phones in their pockets.
- They walk in pairs or in groups and take the most direct route to and from a location.

- They avoid walking through high crime areas.
- They choose to utilize their campus transport or escort services.

As you can see, red flag risk indicators are different depending on the situation and the location. To be able to notice these indicators, you need to be at the appropriate level of awareness. Now that I gave you a few examples, see if you can come up with some on your own by using when-then thinking in your own real-life situation. Think of a time when something didn't go as planned. Were there any signs that things were about to go wrong? If so, what could you have done to prevent them? What would you do differently in the future that could prevent that from happening again?

"While it is important to have a pre-planned, practiced response in mind, if you're not paying attention, you will never see it coming!"

– Gary T. Klugiewicz

Chapter 3
Controlling Your Space and Owning Your Environment

After a long first week of classes, Amanda plopped down on her bed and tried to figure out what she was going to do with her first weekend away from home. She had so much homework she didn't even have time to be homesick, but some of the girls on her floor were getting dressed up to go out. "Come on Amanda! There's a total rager at one of the upper class student houses off campus. EVERYBODY is going," said her friend Brooke. "How is everybody getting there?" Amanda asked. "Oh duh, we're all just going to walk. It's only like eight blocks, and it's so nice out," replied Brooke. Just then, Catie, Kayli, and Maddy all came running into Amanda's room, laughing and ready to party. "Alright let's go you guys," said Kayli. "I've got shots to drink and boys to meet!" "Hahaha... why don't you guys just go ahead? I can meet up with you later. I'm not even dressed yet," said Amanda. "OK girl, we will catch you there," said Catie, as the entire group headed out for the night.

Amanda wasn't really sure about the whole drinking alcohol thing, but she thought it'd still be fun to hang out with the girls and meet new people. She decided to wear a cute new summer dress and sandals, and once she got her make up just right, she headed out for the evening. Within minutes of leaving her dorm, Amanda found herself walking alone on the sidewalk towards a part of campus she had never been. There seemed to be fewer lights than she was used to, and she didn't recognize any of the street names. "This is really creepy... I hope I'm going the right way," she thought, as she frustratingly looked down at her phone to see if her friends had texted her back. When she looked up from her phone she immediately wished she had never took her eyes off of the street. She was suddenly being stared at and followed by two unknown males, who were definitely not college age, and seemed to be whispering to each other as they pointed at her.

A key component of managing your personal safety involves not only evaluating your surroundings, but also managing your space. Amanda went from laughing with her friends and heading out to a party, to finding herself in a very dangerous situation in a mere matter of minutes. During this chapter, I am going to talk about how you can manage your environment so you're safer in it, and also how you can conduct a threat assessment of that space.

But first, I'd like you to think about the place where you feel the safest. This would be a place where you feel completely comfortable, where you feel you could let your guard down, and just chill out. Most people will answer this question and say that they feel the safest at their house. Others will say their bedroom, or their dorm room. For some, it may be at a best friend's house. So let's say you feel the safest in the house you grew up in. There are very good reasons for that. If you have a good relationship with your family, you will find yourself surrounded by love and happiness in your home. There will be no feelings of fear, and you will have a nice warm bed to sleep in at night, and hot food on the table for dinner. Your room will be filled with all of your favorite posters, and you will get to listen to all of your favorite music. In essence, when you are in your home, you feel safe because you know the people in it and you can control the environmental variables that we as humans need to feel safe and comfortable. Now think of a time or a place where you felt the least safe. The answer to this question will vary widely depending on your home environment and your life experiences. To make this point, I will share a story with you.

When I was 20 years old I decided that I was going to fly to New York City to see a concert in Central Park. That sounds pretty cool, right? I was a college sophomore, high on life, and had always wanted to see the city. So I went online and bought a ticket to the concert and I booked myself a flight. For weeks leading up to the concert, it was all I could think about. Three days before my flight, I was already packed and listening to their music non-stop. The day of the trip came and I threw on my favorite pair of jeans, some new Air Maxes, slung my backpack over my shoulder, and jumped on the plane. As the plane was landing in La Guardia, I couldn't wait to get off of it. I will never forget getting off of the plane and walking down the ramp. I had finally made it to New York City.

Knowing nothing about the city and knowing nothing about the taxi services or public transit trains, I decided to ask a friendly looking stranger how I could get to my hotel. He pointed at the train map and mumbled a bunch of numbers, and I figured I was good to go. So I jumped on the "Blue Line 17" train headed towards what I thought was my hotel. And that's when reality kicked in. As I sat down on the train and it started heading "somewhere," I looked around and recognized no one, and nothing. Everybody sitting on the train suddenly looked grumpy and mean, and when they looked at me it seemed like they knew I was a tourist. They looked right through me. Maybe I was being paranoid, but a huge lump started to grow in my throat. I looked outside at all of the graffiti filled buildings. They all had busted windows, and the streets below were littered with trash. This place looked nothing like home. Then the train stopped. The automated message on the overhead speaker told me that this was where I needed to get off. Optimistic, I got off the train and worked my way down the stairs of the platform towards the street.

And then it hit me.

There I was. In the scariest place of my life and the loneliest place I have ever been. It was pitch black out. Not even one street light was working. There was no traffic and no noise. I found myself standing alone, next to a graffiti-riddled brick building, as three very dangerous looking strangers were looking me up and down through their hoods and cigarette smoke. In that moment, I had never been more scared in my life. I was lost and alone. I was unarmed and had no way to defend myself. I felt so threatened for my life that I literally felt my throat close as my hands and feet went numb. I think about it now and all I can do is shake my head. I was so stupid. I could have easily been robbed, or worse, raped. Every time I think of that story, I thank God that an off-duty taxi cab driver had the heart to pull over and help out a lost tourist. "Come here kid. This is not where you want to be," he said. I couldn't get into that cab fast enough, and I was forever grateful to that driver for getting me to my hotel safe. Here's the moral of the story. For as scared as I was, there's a reason I feel so dumb about it now. I was scared out of my mind because I found myself in a time and a place where I had absolutely zero control over my environment, and absolutely no confidence in my ability to defend myself. If only I would have known then what I know now. Let's take a look at the skills that could have prevented that whole situation.

540 Degree Proxemic Management

540 Degree Proxemic Management is a concept developed by several of the Vistelar Consultants, including the Vistelar co-founder Gary Klugiewicz and myself, to describe the skill of actively managing distance and space. If you break it down word by word, intuitively, it

makes sense. The space you need to control isn't just directly in front of you, as you look down at your phone. It includes the 540 degrees that surround you, in front of and behind, left and right, and everything above and below you. This includes all of the potential environmental factors that could come into and/or change that space. This could be the air temperature, the conditions of the walking surface, perhaps a low ceiling or a low hanging shelf, the number of people walking by or how crowded it is. This also includes things like walls, doors, desks and chairs. This could also include cars driving past, how fast they are driving, and if there is a stop sign nearby.

When it comes to understanding proxemics and space management, you have to get creative and really think about all of the factors in that space that change your level of safety in it. Here's a quick example:

> If I were to go for a jog in the park on a nice summer day, most reasonable people would agree that it would be pretty safe in comparison to me running sprints in the street during the middle of winter at night. By jogging in the park in the summer, I wouldn't run the risk of slipping on ice or getting hit by a car. So for this example, I can still *choose* to go for a run, but in evaluating the proxemics of the situation, *one choice would clearly be safer than the other.*

What Are Proxemics?

In the field of communication, "proxemics" refers to the study of non-verbal communication and how distance affects how we communicate with each other. It is the study of the cultural use of space. For our purpose of managing conflict, proxemics refers to where you are positioned in relationship to another person, and how it impacts your ability to safely communicate, both verbally and non-verbally. Remember, we are encouraging you to take ownership of your space, therefore empowering you to stay emotionally and physically safer within that space. So it is imperative that you control your distance, whether it is in relationship to some type of physical hazard or a potentially threatening person.

When you put all of the words together, 540 Degree Proxemic Management includes the evaluation of your 540 degree bubble, so that you can get a full picture of everything that is going on around you. This includes considering your position in relationship to other people (this is also known as relative positioning), as well as assessing barrier options or exit strategies. Barrier options are things like tables, chairs, corners, hills, ditches, and garbage cans: basically anything that you can use to create a barrier, either permanent or temporary, between you and the threat that will help you create time and distance from them. The use of 540 Degree Proxemic Management empowers you to take ownership of all of these aspects of your space.

The 10/5/2 Rule

The 10/5/2 Rule was developed by Vistelar co-founder and nationally known defensive tactics expert Dave Young. People who work in law enforcement and public safety receive a substantial amount of training regarding how to gauge distance in threat assessment. In 1983, law enforcement trainer Dennis Tueller discovered that the average person can cover 21' in less than 1.5 seconds. What this means is that, even if a threat is twenty feet away, you still need to be prepared to react in less than two seconds. For this reason, public safety officials are trained to look far ahead of where they are and keep their eyes constantly moving, in order to give themselves time to react to dangerous situations.

If you don't have that level of training, keeping track of everything 21' feet away can be overwhelming. For your personal life, the 10/5/2 rule was designed to give you a better idea of just how much time and space you need to protect yourself. The farther away a potential threat is from you when you see it, the more time you have to form a plan to either deal with the situation or completely avoid it. Think about driving a car. Do you remember taking your driver's education class? One of the first things they teach you when driving is to look and scan "several seconds" ahead, so that you have time to identify and avoid oncoming problems. This concept is very similar.

To practice the 10/5/2 rule, first take a look around and see if you can accurately judge when something is ten feet away. Then determine what five feet away is, and what is only two feet away. You should measure to make sure that your assessment is accurate!

For this drill, we are going to start our proxemic management at 10', and for this example, we are going to pretend that we are Amanda, who is walking alone at night on the side of the street and suddenly sees two unknown subjects approaching her. If she were practicing good when-then thinking and had an appropriate level of awareness, she would start scanning for potential threats that were 10'-21' feet away from her. In this 10' range, she should be scanning and taking, as Dave Young calls them, "brain pictures" of what is going on around her. To take an accurate brain picture, Amanda should be gathering information with all of her senses. She should be taking mental notes of everything she is seeing, hearing, smelling, and feeling.

Things you should be taking note of at 10' include:
- Looking for possible exit strategies in case you need to escape
- Looking for people who are paying more attention to you than what they are doing
- Looking for how people are interacting with each other, and what they are doing with their hands
- Assessing how fast a person or persons are moving towards you (closing in on your space)

Think: "At 10' I should be surveying the area, assessing people, and evaluating possible exit strategies." The key to this stage is: Evaluate the situation and determine if you should approach or exit.

10' is a safe enough distance that, if you needed to try and completely avoid contact with a suspicious person, you could still avoid them altogether without the risk of being physically attacked. If someone tries to close that space quickly, that's a huge red flag risk indicator!

At 5', the person is about to enter your personal space, and so you need to begin interacting and communicating if you haven't done so already. Because the person is closer, you can hopefully get more information than you could at 10' so that you can better determine what you want to do. Based on what you observe, you might engage the person verbally, or you might begin retreating.

At 5', you should be doing the following things to maintain control of your space:

- Confirming what you saw at 10'. You may be able to better see their hands at 5'

- Checking their body posture, facial expressions, and eye movements

- Getting a better visual of their face, what they're wearing, or what belongings they have with them

- Checking for nervousness or twitching with their hands and feet

Additionally, make eye contact. An aware person looking directly at someone projects to them that you are paying attention and that you've seen them. When appropriate, smile and use the Universal Greeting as they come within speaking distance. We will talk more about the Universal Greeting in Chapter Five.

Think: "At 5' I should be confirming what I saw, is this truly a threat or not? Should I try to communicate with them, or avoid them all together?" The key to this stage is: deciding to communicate or evade.

Remember, just as you are looking for red flags and reading signals from other people, you are also giving them off. While you are scanning to check their body posture, eye movements, and hand movements, they may also be evaluating yours. Part of proxemic management is understanding where you are in relationship to the other person, so you must assess if they are allowing you to keep a safe distance, or if you need to do something to reposition yourself so that you can maintain a safe distance and remain in your comfort zone.

It is important to note here that there are certain traits and conditions that people look for when they decide who their next victim will be. Criminals "pick targets" depending on how "easy" or vulnerable a target looks, or how accessible a place may be to victimization. While I am very careful not to come across as victim blaming, you must realize that there are many risk reduction strategies that you can put in place to make you appear less vulnerable, and therefore, less "victimizable." This includes understanding the signals you are giving off. Do you stand tall, walk with a purpose and with your head up, shoulders back, constantly scanning your surroundings? Or do you slouch over, look apprehensive, and stare at your feet? Do you make direct eye contact with people, or do you constantly avert your eyes when someone approaches you? We want you to recognize how other people perceive you, so that, even if you're in a situation you're apprehensive about, you can still appear confident. It is imperative at this stage that you match up your non-verbal signals with your verbal commands. Basically, we want to make a potential perpetrator go from thinking you are an easy target to thinking you are not someone they want to mess with and that attacking you would be a huge mistake. We will talk more about this in Chapter Five.

Finally, if you find yourself within 2' of a subject, or someone approaches you and is suddenly within that 2' mark, you need to be prepared to act. Think of it like this: if you found yourself this close to someone and the situation suddenly turned physical, you will want to make sure you put yourself in the best position to win the fight. In having this little space to protect yourself, physical danger is much more imminent. You may have to move to get out of the way. You may have to keep your hands above your waist so that you will more quickly be able to protect your face in the event of a sudden assault.

Think: "At 2' I have to position myself in the best place to win, in case this gets physical. I may also have to escape." The key to this stage is taking action and keeping them out of your personal danger zone. You may have to: Operate or escape.

In the event that you fear for your physical safety and you're being attacked, you may have to get physical and defend yourself. Obviously, the first thing you should try to do is escape, or disengage from the situation. It is a natural human reaction to freeze, and then backpedal away from a threat. A good rule of thumb to remember is never take more than two steps backwards. If you start to take three, four, or five steps backwards, you will likely lose your balance, or run into something or someone that you were unable to see behind you. Try to move in an "L" shape, by taking only a couple steps backwards, and then side stepping to the safest side so that you can regain your balance and move yourself off to the side and away from the assailant's forward momentum. This is also known as "getting off of the tracks."

Think: "Get out of the way of an oncoming train. If I ran straight down the tracks, it would still hit me. All I have to do is step off of them."

Remember, I am not encouraging you to go around and start picking fights with people. In fact that is the exact opposite of what I'm suggesting. I am presenting you with strategies you can use in case the "fight comes to you." If you do have to get physical, you should use self-defense moves, improvised weapons, and barrier options to help you create distance from your attacker. You should use trained self-defense techniques to try and affect their breathing, impair their vision, create pain, and most importantly, to create distance from your attacker so that you can escape and seek out help. It is in this type of situation where you may be scared of your surroundings. By using these strategies, you will start thinking more about how to use your surroundings to your advantage. Criminals hate places with more light, more sound, and more noise. Here, in a life or death situation, you will need to think unconventionally, so that you can defend yourself and start drawing more attention to you. Dave Young, defensive tactics expert and Vistelar co-founder, uses this example:

> If you're running through a parking lot and trying to seek safety inside the store, don't be afraid to push on or run on a few cars to set off the car alarms. Make sure you're scanning for easily grabbable improvised weapons or "weapons of opportunity" that you could use to defend yourself. Now this doesn't mean just running through the parking lot and grabbing the first thing you see, such as a garbage can, *it means searching for an impact tool that falls within your ability to use it.* In other words, grabbing the first thing you see may not be the best option to defend your-self because it may be too heavy and too bulky, but it could potentially be flipped over and used as a barrier to help you create some time and distance between you and your assailant. This would give you more time to search for something you're better able to defend yourself with, such as a fire extinguisher, club, or brick.

One of the concepts Vistelar teaches is that there is a huge difference between "fire drills" and "fire talks." There is a reason that schools across America have adopted mandatory fire drill training, and not just fire related education in the classroom setting. If and when a fire does happen, we want children and teachers to have physically practiced what to do, instead of just knowing what to do, or thinking about what to do. The same goes for the skills and concepts discussed throughout this book. You need to practice these skills so you can become confident and can execute them when you need it.

"There are two types of people in the world. Those that THINK or HOPE 'it will never happen to me,' and those that will BE READY, when it does."

– Dave Young

Chapter 4
A Practical Approach to Threat Assessment

Amanda kept a close eye on the two unknown individuals that had now been following her for several blocks. She noticed that they were closing in on her, and that one of them kept holding his hand on the beltline of his pants, as if he was trying to hide something or hold something. She felt her heart start to race and her palms get sweaty, so she quickened her pace and turned left at the next block. "Jordan!" she screamed, as she ran towards her and hugged her.

Jordan was with several people Amanda didn't recognize, but she couldn't be happier. "Dude, Amanda, you don't even like me. What's your deal?" said Jordan. As she looked up, she noticed the two creepy looking individuals who had been following Amanda. They had stopped, turned around, and started walking away. "Oh," she said. "That could've gone bad. Let's get you to where you were headed. Stick with us." Amanda may not have been friends with Jordan, but boy, was she thankful to run into her.

Up to this point, you have learned a lot of new information about how to manage your space and how to keep yourself safer within that space. You have learned:

• How to be a when-then thinker

- Conditions of Awareness

- How to identify red flag risk indicators

- 540 Degree Proxemic Management and the 10/5/2 rule

Now, we are going to further discuss what to look for in various situations you will encounter on campus. First, we need to understand the difference between threat assessment and risk assessment.

At its most basic level, "risk assessment" can be understood as a systematic process of evaluating what risks you are vulnerable to. For example, if you went sky diving, you are vulnerable to serious injury because your parachute could fail. If you had a leg injury, you would now be more vulnerable to having someone steal your wallet and run away with it because you would be less able to catch them. After you have identified vulnerabilities, you can take measures to reduce them. Next, you should conduct a threat assessment, which involves identifying any threats to those vulnerabilities. If your parachute had a broken string—that's a huge threat! If you saw someone tailing you on the street, that person could pose a theft threat. Both of these skills are important. You need to be able to identify your vulnerabilities accurately so you know what risks you might face, and you need to be aware of the elements in your environment that pose threats to those vulnerabilities.

Threat assessment in a given situation, or of a specific person, is a continuous process. It isn't something you do "just one time," and then you automatically assume since something was safe a few minutes ago, that it is safe now. For example, let's say you needed to cross a busy street. There is the risk that you could get hit by a car. So to prevent yourself from getting hit by the car, you seek out a cross walk, and wait for a red light, which helps you minimize the risk of getting hit by a car. Then you look both ways before stepping into the road. By looking both ways before you cross the street, you made a threat assessment of the situation and decided either to cross the street, or wait for cars to pass. But let's say last week you had to cross the same intersection, and you looked both ways and it was safe to cross, so you did. That doesn't mean that this week you'd just blindly walk up to the intersection and step into the road. You would look both ways again to determine if it was safe, and even as you continued to cross the road you would continue to look both ways to make sure a speeding car doesn't run a red light and hit you. In a nutshell, this is how you should approach the ongoing threat assessment process in every situation.

Conducting a Threat Assessment

So now that you know what threat assessment is, I'm going to go into more detail about how to do it. One of the first things you need to think about is how vulnerable you are in a particular situation. If you needed to get home late at night after studying, you'd be less vulnerable to robbery or assault if you were in a car rather than walking. If you needed to walk, you'd be less vulnerable to robbery or assault if you were practicing good 540 Degree Proxemic management, had your valuables hidden, and were wearing practical footwear, rather than walking alone, intoxicated, texting on your smartphone, and wearing flip flops. All of those little things contribute to your overall vulnerability in a situation. To assess vulnerability, you also need to consider, "What is the source of the threat I am vulnerable to, and why?" If you can answer those questions, you will be well equipped to protect yourself against it. Remember, the more distracted you are within your environment, the more vulnerable you are to it!

There are many threat assessment opportunities for you to consider. Again, if you walk into a situation and something or someone just doesn't feel right, listen to it. Your gut instinct is telling you to go from Condition Yellow to Condition Orange, and whatever it was that set off your radar deserves your attention. Some of the things you should consider when conducting a threat assessment of a person include:

- The time of day, your location, and if you are around other people, sound, and light.

- The relative age, size, strength, and skill level of the potential threat(s).

- If they are "enjoying their space," or focused on you or another person.

- If they have rapid breathing and seem anxious or nervous (fidgety).

- If they make an unexpected movement or change direction and head directly toward you.

- If they start to increase their level of movement or start to exaggerate their movements.

- If they appear to go from calm to angry, and start showing excessive signs of emotional distress.

In the example above, Amanda started to take notice of several of these things. She noticed that it was late at night (dark), she was alone (outnumbered), the subjects pointed at her (were more focused on her than what they were doing), and started heading directly towards her (unexpected change in direction). Do you remember what else Amanda noticed? That's right. One of the subjects grabbed the waistband of his pants as if he was holding something up. Could it have been a handgun? It very possibly could have!

People who are about to attack you will also give away other clues. You should be able to notice a change in their body posture—they will assume a more "athletic" stance, also known as a "boxer" stance, and you may even be able to see them start clenching their fists and shifting their shoulders in an effort to get into a more powerful position to attack you. These are all indications that you should be managing your space, and doing everything you can to create more distance between you and that individual.

Assessing a New Campus

You have learned many new skills up to this point. At the very least, you should be seeing your world differently and learning how to take your safety into your own hands. Let's put some of your new knowledge to the test and pretend it is your first day on campus, a brand new environment. You are still with your parents; they've helped you unload your stuff, set up your room, and want to take you out for dinner before they head home many, many miles away. Your mom, a lifelong police officer, smirks and asks you, "So, have you figured out the safest way to get to all of your classes yet?" You laugh, but you suddenly realize that she isn't kidding, and you start to look around. "Don't worry mom, I already have my whole safety plan laid out!" Your mom smiles, "Ok then, let's hear it."

Using the skills you have learned, take a quick risk assessment of your campus. Try to outline situations or circumstances where you'd be the most vulnerable to crime. This would be a great exercise to practice with your parents and your friends too.

Since it's your first time, I will help you out. Here is a checklist of some of the things you should do as soon as you get to your new campus:

- Colleges have highly trained professionals presenting orientation sessions. ATTEND them and LISTEN! As difficult as it will be with all of the excitement to stop meeting new people and talking to new friends, you must take advantage of the information they are giving you. That information will help protect you and make you less vulnerable to crime in the future.

- Identify where your campus security/police department is

located. Do they have substations? Do they offer safety training or self-defense classes throughout the year? If they do, recruit some of your friends and take one!

• Put the campus security/police number in your cell phone, and make sure you label it with an easily recallable name in case of a high stress emergency.

• Do they have blue light or emergency phones and surveillance cameras? I bet your campus security loves to show them off— find out if they have brochures on the locations of the phones, or better yet, ask to do a ride along so you can learn more about what they do, and where the safe (and more dangerous) areas are on campus.

• Figure out on a map where your dorm room is in relationship to your classes. Locate the safest route to and from them. This may not mean the "shortest" route, and it may not mean that it's the same route to and from. For example, if you have a Thursday night class from 7-9:40 pm, it may be safe to take a shortcut through several alleys to get there, but at 9:40 pm at night, it may be smarter to take a main campus thoroughfare that is well traveled, well lit, and passes several emergency phones. Do the same assessment for walking to and from your favorite study spots, restaurants, and hangouts, taking notice of the street names- campuses look very different at night!

• Does your campus have a transportation service? Use it! And not just when it's cold or raining. Most campuses offer safety shuttles of some kind that will safely take you all over campus.

• Make sure all of your expensive belonging are identifiable if stolen, such as music players, cell phones, laptops, and bikes etc. Borrow an engraver or check with your campus security to see if they have one.

- Make sure your parents know your class schedule and what types of debit and credit cards you keep in your purse/wallet. Keep your bank information handy, so that you can cancel your cards quickly if they are stolen.

I realize that these things may seem trivial or unnecessary, but in the event of something happening to you or your belongings, this small amount of preparation could be a matter of life or death!

"There are things you can do to keep yourself safer. Don't go through life just hoping that bad things won't happen. Hope is not a tactic."

Jill Weisensel

Chapter 5
Communication Tactics for Campus Life

Amanda walked into the party, still shook up from the walk over. She couldn't believe what had happened, and was scared to think about what would have happened if she hadn't run into Jordan. The party was packed. The music was so loud that the bass was vibrating the pictures on the wall, and it even knocked a few onto the floor that was covered with beer and red solo cups. Everyone was shouting and laughing and doing something different. Some were dancing, some were playing a drinking game she had never seen before, and several people were out front lighting off fireworks. "Ouch," she said, as she got run into by two guys who were play fighting. "Whoa, my bad 'bout that girly. Haven't seen you before...freshman?" Said one of the guys. "Hi, I'm Paul, and that's Brian. Have a drink!" Paul handed her a red solo cup filled to the brim that smelled awful- it was some concoction of booze and juice, one that Amanda had no intention of drinking. "Nah guys, thanks... but I don't drink. You drink it." And almost as fast as she said it, it seemed the music stopped and everyone stopped and stared at her in disbelief. "She doesn't... drink?" Said one. "Ha, well she does now!" Said another, as she pointed towards several people trying to grab her. "To the keg then! Congrats freshman, you're about to complete your first keg stand!" Amanda was terrified, and suddenly found herself being drug into the kitchen by several people she didn't know.

41

So far, this entire book has been dedicated to personal safety awareness, and what you can do to evaluate your environment and stay safer in it. Now that you know how to manage your space and how to identify and avoid threats, we are going to completely shift gears and look at several communication strategies. These communication strategies are meant to be used in tandem with all of the physical skills you just learned about. As mentioned before, you must mesh the verbal and non-verbal skills together in order to avoid conflict and defuse it. Unfortunately, conflict may come to you when you least expect it, just as it did for Amanda. I couldn't write a book about campus safety without including the communication skills necessary to try and prevent situations from becoming physical. In fact, if you look at law enforcement statistics, you will find that the majority of all law enforcement encounters end without having to use force. If cops, firefighters, teachers, and nurses can use these communication skills to manage conflict and maintain their safety during extremely stressful circumstances, so can you.

It All Starts With Respect

At Vistelar, we believe that one of the best ways to manage conflict between people is to identify and recognize the things that all people have in common. In the middle of a conflict, it is important to recognize how you'd like the conflict to end, and if you see someone else getting into an argument or in an uncomfortable position, you should try and put yourself into their shoes, and see the situation through their eyes. This demonstrates empathy, and it is a highly useful tool in figuring out the most respectful way to resolve a situation. In the previous scenario, Amanda just found herself in a horribly awkward position, and she may not be able to get out of it unless she can convince the partygoers to change their behavior. Unless one (or more) of her friends decides to step up and intervene, Amanda will have to talk her way out of it.

Vistelar teaches this core principle of conflict management: treat people with dignity by showing respect. Over the last thirty-plus years of working with almost every profession, Vistelar has learned that treating people with dignity just works better in managing conflict and had identified these five approaches to showing respect.

- See the world through their eyes

- "Listen" with all of your senses

- Ask and explain why

- Offer options, let them choose

- Give opportunity to reconsider

These five approaches describe how all people want to be treated. Everyone wants to be shown empathy, listened to, asked to do something rather than told to do it, be provided with an explanation for why they are being asked, offered options from which they can choose, and given an opportunity to rethink a decision. It is important to understand that Vistelar does not teach that you need to respect everyone. That would be impossible, since respect is based on your personal values and must be earned. However, it is essential – if you want to be effective at conflict management – that you show everyone respect. All people deserve to be shown respect.

To see the world through the other persons' eyes and to listen with all of your senses, is the starting point for any successful interaction. If you aren't paying attention to what a person says, observing what they do, and noticing how they respond, you won't be able to persuade them to cooperate or collaborate with you. Vistelar emphasizes listening with all of your senses because there's a lot more to notice than just what someone says. We'll get into this skill more when we talk about Beyond Active Listening later in the chapter.

Let's use our example above, and pretend that an onlooker at the party was paying attention enough to notice that Amanda was terrified of having to do a keg stand. That onlooker would have been listening with all the senses—not just hearing what was happening, but seeing the fear on Amanda's face, feeling her worry about how to handle the peer pressure, and empathizing with her desire to get out of that situation.

When just listening isn't enough to resolve the situation, you need to speak up. Approach three (ask and explain why) works off of the human desire to know "why" we are being asked to do something. Think of a small child who is begging his mommy or daddy for some candy at the store. The parents say, "No, you can't have any candy right now." What's the first thing the toddler says? "Why? Why mommy why?" The usual response you hear from the parent is "because I said so," which usually results in the toddler asking "why" again, several more times. We know that you are more likely to persuade someone to do something if you ask them to do it, rather than order them to do it, and you may even be able to get them to do it willingly, if you can explain to them why it is important or in their best interest to do so. Lots of times people in authority believe the question "why" is a question against their authority. It isn't. Being able to give people the answer is actually empowering!

To continue with our onlooker: imagine if this person walked up to the guys "playfully" dragging her and said, "Let her go now! This is stupid." That sentence is a command, and would most likely generate resistance from the group. However, if the friendly onlooker came up to the group and said, "Hey guys, could you please not force her to do that? I really don't want her puking on all of our stuff later." The onlooker is now treating the group with respect. Which approach is more likely to get a positive result?

And if they didn't let her go and would've responded with

laughter and told the helpful bystander to get lost? They could then use approaches four and five, and offer the guys options and an opportunity to make things right. They could then say, "Look, I realize you guys are just trying to have a good time, but this clearly isn't fun for her. What do you say we let her go so we can get back to having a good time? I'd hate to see her get drunk and sick and then tell the campus police tomorrow that people were drinking underage. What do you think?"

The dialogue used by our interventionist is also known as a "Persuasion Sequence." The Persuasion Sequence works hand in hand with Vistelar's five approaches to showing people respect, and you are already starting to see how effective it can be. We will learn more about the Persuasion Sequence a little later on.

The Showtime Mindset

Another Vistelar concept is adopting a "Showtime Mindset." Showtime helps us remember that the entire world is a stage, and that people perceive us differently than we perceive ourselves. Think of a time when you spent a lot of time getting ready before going out, and you took one last look in the mirror and thought "Man, I'm looking goooood." Then right before you walk out the door one of your parents said to you "You're not leaving the house looking like that... are you?" The idea behind the Showtime Mindset is that the way you present yourself matters for communication, so you should adopt an attitude that projects confidence and self-assurance.

Remember in Chapter Three when I said that it is imperative for your non-verbal behavior to match your verbalizations? What you say has to match how you say it, and what you look like saying it. Research has shown that the majority of what we communicate is delivered through our *delivery style*. This means that the message we are trying to deliver, at any given time, is delivered mostly through our non-verbal mannerisms, and the pace, pitch, and modulation of our voice. Very little of the message we deliver is in the content of the actual words. So, if you say the exact same thing, but deliver it in a different way, it actually means something different. The skill of Showtime is being conscious of the presence we project through our non-verbals and our tone, so that people will believe the words we use.

Sometimes it is hard not to let our body language give away our true feelings. Have you ever had a really bad day and your mom asks you what's wrong and knows something's wrong even though you said you're fine? A Showtime Mindset helps you guard against that by allowing you to put all of the negative things in your life aside just long enough so you can step up, appear confident, and handle the task at hand.

Think about a basketball player on a free throw line. You can easily tell which players are super confident and look like they will make the shot, versus the ones who appear scared and unsure of themselves. You've probably also noticed when a friend has a really bad day at school, and then they play a really bad game. Ever notice how some people can have a really bad day at school and then still somehow manage to play an awesome game? That's because they are able to mentally turn off one version of themselves (the student version) and turn on the athlete version. Showtime is a complete mental shift, allowing you to put other things aside, and appear confident, even if you're not. Sometimes in conflict, you have to fake it until you make it, and put on the face you need to succeed.

To help you understand how you appear to others, I want to introduce the "Less Than, Greater Than, Equal To" drill to help teach the point of appearing passive, assertive, or aggressive. This drill was developed by Vistelar Consultant and martial arts trainer Master Chan Lee to help school kids protect themselves from bullying. In this drill, you think about the first 5-10 seconds that a new person meets you. During that time, they will make a quick determination to assess if they are "greater than you, less than you, or equal to you," and based upon that designation, they will treat you as such. Now this sounds somewhat superficial, but as a concept, you can see it with how people talk to each other: people who think they are "greater than" someone else, tend to talk down to other people, command them, and use a condescending tone. These people will also "puff up" their postures, increase their gait, hold their head high and start acting like they are better than other people. These types of people become bullies. People who naturally feel "less than," will tend to "shrink" their posture, avert their eyes, act passively, and speak meekly. These types of people become bullied.

What does "equal to" look like? It looks like confidence without being overbearing. If you show yourself as "equal to", you will stand up straight; you won't be hunched over or sticking your chest out. You will look the other person in the eye—not staring them down, but also not avoiding their gaze. When you speak, your voice will be calm and will be at an appropriate volume, neither whispering nor shouting.

The purpose of this exercise is to be specific about what confidence looks like, so you can project it even when you're not feeling it. The concept shows us that it is possible to "up sell" our posture. Therefore, you can become a less desirable target for bullying, harassment, or victimization. We want you to do everything you can to prevent yourself from becoming a target, while also recognizing that if something bad does happen to you, it isn't your fault. As mentioned earlier, the only person who can actually prevent the crime from happening is the person committing it.

Emotional Equilibrium

Talking your way out of conflict is a real life skill, and we realize that it isn't a natural thing to do. At Vistelar we teach many communication concepts that can help make the art of talking out of conflict easier for you. One of the concepts is Emotional Equilibrium. This concept is a complex one, but at its most basic level, it will help you identify and protect against the emotions that make it difficult for you to keep your cool and communicate under pressure during a seriously awkward or confrontational situation.

Think of a time that you were really angry and you got into a fight with your best friend. You notice how hard it was to say exactly what you meant, and exactly what you were upset about? That's because people rarely say what they mean when they are upset. This means we must try to stay calm so that we can respond to their meaning, rather than react to their exact words. Emotional Equilibrium encourages you to maintain a "still center," recognizing that in times of conflict you must stay calm, breath, and have your emotions—not "be" them. This means that even when you're angry or frustrated in an argument you will be able to control your emotions, rather than have your emotions control you, so that you will remain clear headed enough to make good decisions.

In order to maintain your Emotional Equilibrium, you have to take some time to recognize your weaknesses—those things that are likely to set you off and make you really angry. Everybody has "hot buttons" that really makes their blood boil. It is important that you identify what makes you angry and know how you react to them, so that you are prepared to respond appropriately when someone says it to you. For example, one of my hot buttons is having my opinion blown off by someone, who doesn't know anything about me or my level of experience, just because I'm a female. I have worked very hard my entire career to remain physically and mentally fit by pursuing additional training opportunities, and seeking out advanced education. Essentially, I have worked my whole life to become technically proficient and competent at my job, and that has nothing to do with being female. Because I have worked hard to maintain my skills, I have developed an "Emotion Guard" to keep me from becoming angry when someone disrespects me. My Emotion Guard allows me to project a strong, confident, and unphased image, and it protects me from displaying emotions that I may not want to share with other people.

I have found it extremely useful to adopt the Showtime Mindset in order to maintain Emotional Equilibrium. Conceptually, the two go hand in hand. I know that even if I'm having a bad day at home, I need to put aside all of my problems when I go to work. I'm a supervisor, and if I drag my personal issues into the workplace, it is likely that they will also drag down my crew. Having the Showtime Mindset allows me to go to work and temporarily put all of the negative things in my life on hold, so that I can better perform for my team. By maintaining my Emotional Equilibrium, and remaining cool, calm and collected, my crew is better equipped to do their job, knowing that I'm capable of doing mine even under the most stressful circumstances.

The Universal Greeting

Are you generally shy and nervous to talk to new people? Do you have a friend who just seems like they can talk to anyone, and they make it look easy? There are many skills that you can learn that can help you get through the awkwardness of talking to new people. In light of treating all people with dignity and respect, we teach a communication tactic called the Universal Greeting. The Universal Greeting is a standard, pre-planned way of initiating a conversation with someone that will help you set the stage for a positive interaction. The components of the Universal Greeting are:

- Use an appropriate greeting, such as "Good morning," or "Excuse me."

- Introduce yourself and your affiliation, such as "I'm Keith Jones, and I live down the hallway."

- Explain the reason you're talking with them, such as "We're hosting a dorm meet and greet spaghetti dinner as a fundraiser."

- Ask a relevant question, such as "Would you be interested in buying tickets?"

Using the Universal Greeting makes initiating that first, somewhat awkward contact a lot easier, and it sets the stage for a better outcome because you appear confident and courteous. The Universal Greeting allows you to state the reason for why you're talking with them and makes sure that both individuals engaging in the conversation know what the conversation is actually about. Another benefit of introducing yourself this way, is that it aligns seamlessly with the Persuasion Sequence, in the event that they say "no" to your question or generate some sort of resistance to your inquiry. I will show you how to put both of these skills together in the Bystander Intervention chapter.

Beyond Active Listening

Now that you've identified your hot buttons and found a way to stay calm and appear calm under pressure, we are going to talk about going Beyond Active Listening—developing skills that will allow you to truly hear what other people are saying. Other people teach active listening skills, and that's a good start, but to be effective you have to go beyond just "active listening." Fully understanding another person's message requires more than just hearing what someone is saying—you must truly listen to their side of the story and be open and unbiased. Vistelar Consultant Doug Lynch, explains it like this:

"There is a difference between hearing and listening. It is the difference between acknowledging and understanding. Between reacting and responding. Let me share a brief example. Driving back from a presentation in Prescott, Arizona to my home in Phoenix, while coming down a twisting mountain highway, a loud metallic bang emitted from under the rear of my truck. It was time to quickly pull over and examined the vehicle very closely. This stretch of road combining: highway speeds, small guardrails and hundred foot drop offs is not the place you want to lose control of your vehicle. Finding nothing obviously wrong and having no cell phone signal to call for help, I started back down the road but, now, attentive to every sound coming from the truck. In anticipation of a further problem, both hands were placed firmly on the wheel alert to any unusual vibrations in the vehicle, the radio was turned off and I slowed my driving pace to the minimum speed limit. If something started to malfunction, I was in a better place to guide the vehicle safely to the shoulder of the highway. I was now listening to the vehicle until arriving safely at home. Hearing something can force a reaction, listening to something helps you to form a response. In human conflict, this can be the difference between reaching peaceful resolution and not."

In this scenario, Lynch was hyper-vigilant about what was happening with his car. He was paying attention for anything that might have indicated a problem—an unexpected vibration, an unusual sound, even the smell of something burning or leaking. When we approach a situation with potential conflict, we need to be as tuned in to what the other person is communicating. As I mentioned before, people rarely ever say what they mean when they are upset, so if you were only listening with your ears, you will most undoubtedly fail to hear their message. Beyond Active Listening means also "listening" with your eyes so that you can observe their body language, non-verbal cues, voice tone, and their distance from you. When you are listening to someone, your goal isn't just to "get the facts." Your goal is to truly understand the context of their situation. If you find yourself having trouble understanding the meaning of a difficult conversation, use these steps:

- Ask To Clarify: Use skillful questioning to clarify what the person believes, as well as why they hold those beliefs.

- Paraphrase: Put their meaning into your words to ensure understanding. Paraphrasing provides an opportunity to ensure that what you heard is what the other person intended to communicate.

- Reflect: If you need to interrupt, start with "Can I ask a question to see if I understand?" Then state your view of what the other person is feeling and why – and ask if you are correct.

- Mirror: Subtly imitate the other person's subconscious body orientation, posture, mannerisms, eye contact, tone of voice and talking pace, but never his or her negative body language. This helps build rapport, trust, and liking so the other person is more open to communicating with you.

- Advocate: Acknowledge the issue and express how you and the other person should work together to address it, for example, say "That sounds like a big problem; let's work together to figure out how to fix it."

- Summarize: Use a summarizing statement to make sure everyone agrees with what has been said so you can move forward towards resolution.

The first technique, empathizing, means attempting to understand how the other person is experiencing the situation. Empathy is a challenging skill because you are trying to imagine what is going on inside another person's head, and often you don't have the full picture. For instance, you may not know that your roommate just got her first "F" and her fear is affecting your conversation. But, you can recognize that your roommate is more on edge than usual, and you can genuinely try to understand her perspective. When you empathize with your roommate, you acknowledge that something is amiss. As a result, you can ask, "Is there something else bothering you right now?" instead of plowing ahead with your complaints about the dirty dishes in your room.

The second technique, asking questions to clarify, helps establish common ground in the conversation. When done well, asking questions also shows that you are genuinely interested in what the other person is thinking. When combined with empathy, asking questions to clarify helps defuse confrontational situations because the techniques demonstrate an openness to hear what the other person thinks. In order to ask questions well, it is important to choose questions that don't put the other person on the defensive. The way you ask the question matters. There are five generally understood ways to ask a question:

- Fact-finding: This is good for acquiring specific information or data, and has a neutral effect on the respondent. If you ask too many fact finding questions in a row you could appear unempathetic.

- General: This would be an open ended question, such as, "What's going on here now?" This lets the responder answer the way she or he chooses, and because they can choose their response, it makes them feel good.

- Opinion-seeking: Everyone loves to give their opinion. Asking a question such as, "What's the best way to solve this problem?" displays empathy and could give you much more valuable information than just fact finding questions alone.

- Direct: These questions require as simple "yes" or "no" answer. They are useful in moderation for focusing the discussion, but like fact finding questions, this could make a person feel interrogated or cornered if done repeatedly.

- Leading: These questions tend to anger respondents, as they feel they are being pressured a certain way and it appears that you already have your mind made up regarding the answer.

A third tool you have available during a confrontational discussion is paraphrasing. Paraphrasing allows you to put another person's meaning into your own words, and state it back to them to ensure you understood their meaning correctly. If a person is going on and on and you are having a hard time figuring out their point, paraphrase is a good tool because it forces the speaker to pause long enough to make sure you're understanding them. Generally speaking, this results in the speaker modifying what they originally said, because they will realize they were upset and didn't say exactly what they meant.

Paraphrase also allows you to "interrupt" someone and not upset them, as if you were trying to cut them off as they were speaking. You can simply say, "Hold on. Let me make sure I understand what you just said." That will force the speaker to pause and give you a second to process what they were saying so you can make sure you understood it. Doing this also shows the other person that you are in fact listening to them, and that displays empathy!

Finally, summarizing ensures that both parties are on the same page. After you have empathized with the other person, asked questions to clarify their position, and used paraphrase to make sure you understood what they meant to communicate, you still need to move forward—either towards a resolution, or into another tactic like the Persuasion Sequence. A summary is a brief statement of how the situation stands. When you finish summarizing, both parties should understand what each other is thinking.

The Persuasion Sequence

The Persuasion Sequence is another pre-planned communication tactic that will help you persuade others and generate cooperation. This communication method is a critical conflict resolution skill. Just as the Universal Greeting ended with "ask a relevant question," the Persuasion Sequence picks up with what to do if you "ask" someone to do something, and they say "no," or refuse to respond or change their unacceptable behavior. The need to persuade people usually starts with someone requesting cooperation of another person. Then, if the person questions, resists for refuses the request, the Persuasion Sequence can be used as follows:

- Explain why you are asking them to do something and confirm their understanding. You can do this by providing your explanation and telling them why your explanation is valid. Then ask if they understand your explanation.

- If they continue to not cooperate, then you would offer them options and let them choose. Present a vivid description of a positive option and then a negative option. Tell them it is their choice and ask again for their cooperation. Make sure when you do this you use a friendly and cooperative tone so as not to come across threatening.

- Give them the opportunity, one more time, to reconsider their behavior.
  If the other person has not cooperated after this third step,

your options for Taking Appropriate Action will vary depending on the situation.

Taking Appropriate Action could mean following through on the options you presented, or taking the next best course of action. In a less serious situation, such as an argument with your roommate, the appropriate action might be to decide that it's not worth pursuing the issue further. In more serious situations, you might call for help or find a way to leave the situation.

Let's put this into our keg stand scenario from earlier. A bystander stepped up and tried to help Amanda from getting dragged into the kitchen to do a keg stand. The bystander verbally set the context of the situation for the subjects, and then offered options to them, stating, "Look, I realize you guys are just trying to have a good time, but this clearly isn't fun for her. What do you say we let her go so we can get back to having a good time? I'd hate to see her get drunk and sick and then tell the campus police tomorrow that people were drinking underage. What do you think?" If the guys were to respond with, "Nah, this is more fun anyways," our interventionist could then say, "Is there anything I can say to you guys so you will leave her alone?" And if not, the interventionist will have exhausted all of their verbal options and will have to follow through with some sort of action (act).

In this case, an appropriate course of action could be to talk to the party host and let them know that they are forcing underage students to drink. It could also be enlisting a couple more friends to help get her out of there (literally "tag teaming" to remove her from the situation). Ultimately, this situation could also result in calling campus security to resolve the issue.

The Persuasion Sequence is highly effective if used properly. You must make sure to set the full context of the situation, so that you can present people with options. When you appropriately set context for people you "change the reality of the event" for them, as it changes their perspective. When you give someone perspective (perspective giving) it forces them to rethink the position of the other person (perspective taking), and will most likely result in an empathy-driven change of behavior.

Tip: Drawing a blank trying to set the context? Think about what the person has to gain from the situation going well or what they'd have to lose from the situation going badly. If presented tactfully, this reality check could provide just the right amount of perspective they need to change their behavior. Some trainers refer to this concept as "WII F.M."... the "radio station that everyone listens to." It stands for "What's In It For Me." If you can explain to someone how they'd benefit from a situation, they are likely to cooperate!

Redirecting an Argument

No matter how well intended your conversation is, people still may come at you with verbal resistance. People don't like to be told what to do, and if you're asking them to change their behavior, they may in fact "verbally assault" you. The first thing you need to do is keep calm, and remember Emotional Equilibrium, Showtime Mindset, and your hot-button Emotion Guards. But just because you've managed to keep your cool, doesn't mean that the other person will. If you continue to get verbally assaulted and you say nothing to address the situation, you will eventually get angry and leave, or get angry and start screaming back at the other person. Another communication tactic that we teach involves using certain pre-planned phrases that are non-escalatory to deal with a verbal assault. Vistelar calls this tactic, "Redirections." You can also think of this tactic as "word blocks" — defensive shields to protect yourself from verbal assaults.

Redirections have two steps: 1) acknowledge the tactic and 2) move past the attack and either get back on point or leave.

Here are a few examples:

- "I appreciate that, however . . ."

- "I understand that; however. . ."

- "I hear that, and. . ."

- "I got that; however. . ."

- "I'm sorry you feel that way, and . . ."

- "Unfortunately, someone gave you some bad information."

- "I can understand why you're angry and under the same circumstances I would probably be angry too. However…"

- "I can understand that you don't like me and that's OK, but if we get into an argument here… we both lose."

Note that, in all these examples, the attack is acknowledged but it isn't addressed. With a Redirection, your message to the other person is that a) you have heard them, b) their attack has no impact on you and c) the interaction must be focused on your agenda, not theirs.

One time I got into huge argument with my best friend. She was really upset and started yelling at me, and she was so upset that she wasn't really telling me what she was angry about. I was able to get her to stop yelling by saying, "I can see that you're angry, except I can't help you if you don't stop yelling." That sentence was just enough to get her to stop and think about what she was saying. She then said, "I'm sorry, I'm not angry with you. You're just the only one here." That made me a feel a lot better.

Precision of Word Choice

The less time you have to communicate a message, such as in a bystander intervention situation, the more critical it is that you mean what you say, and you say exactly what you mean. One word can make all the difference! This means you need to articulate and remember "Precision of Word Choice."

Precision of Word Choice simply reminds you to be mindful that even a slight change in word choice can drastically change the meaning of an intended message, as words can mean very different things to different people, as a result of prior experiences, biases, and assumptions. You can clearly see how much a single word can change your meaning by trying a word association drill. Test several of your friends. Tell them that you are going to pick a word, and when you say the word out loud, you want them to tell you the first thing that comes to their mind when they hear it. Try using a word like "fast" or "pizza." You will be shocked by how many different answers you get! Understanding how words are interpreted differently by other people will help you choose the exactly right words you need in any given situation. Because word choice matters so much, it is important to use when-then thinking and plan out what you would say in a confrontational situation. How would you ask your roommate to turn down the music? How would you support one of your friends who was being pressured to drink? The reason we script out tactics like the Universal Greeting and the Persuasion Sequence is so you can find the right words easily when you need them.

This chapter just serves as an introduction to these important communication skills. Just like any other physical skill, such as hitting a baseball or shooting a basketball, these skills take practice. I highly encourage you to practice these skills any chance you get, and use the online companion to this book to access many additional training resources to help you improve your communication skill set.

"The single biggest problem with communication is the illusion that it has taken place."

– George Bernard Shaw

Chapter 6

The Concept of Bystander Intervention

Amanda stood in the kitchen surrounded by at least thirty people, and she didn't recognize a single one. Paul and Brian were trying to set up the keg and she realized she was going to have to drink or risk getting made fun of for the whole rest of the night. Desperately, she looked around the room to see if anyone cared...if anyone cared at all that she didn't want to drink. "Outnumbered thirty to one," she thought, "This isn't going to end well...my parents are going to kill me." Amanda looked up, and her eyebrows rose slightly. Jordan had just walked in, looked at her, and shook her head in disgust. Jordan looked at Amanda, looked at the crowd, and then looked carefully at Brian and Paul. "Now what?" Jordan thought.

Jordan was faced with a tough decision at a critical point in time. She could join in the (not) "fun" and force Amanda to drink, or she could help her get out of there and risk being shunned by her peers. Unfortunately, this is a scenario that plays out over and over again on college campuses.

Now that you have learned about concepts such as the Conditions of Awareness, 540 Degree Proxemic Management (for safety), Beyond Active Listening (for information gathering), and the Universal Greeting, Persuasion Sequence, and Redirections (for de-escalating conflict), you have been exposed to all of the skill sets you will need to recognize situations that are going badly and require intervention. You see, "bystanders" actually comprise of the largest number of people in the cycle of violence. Let me put that statement into perspective. If we look at the social cycles of discrimination, bullying, harassment, alcohol abuse, physical abuse, and on up through sexual violence, the number of people, in terms of a percentage, that are actually "perpetrators" of the behavior or are direct "victims" as a result of the behavior, is actually very small in comparison to the number of people who are "bystanders" to the behavior.

Concepts of bystander intervention and ethical intervention are well understood as they pertain to law enforcement and security professionals. They are also commonly understood by managers, supervisors, and disturbance resolution specialists. It's easy to "sell the need" for bystander intervention strategies to people in positions of power. People in positions of authority generally realize that they SHOULD act and that they have a professional responsibility to act.

It's a whole different story though when trying to convince the average student, employee, or citizen to intervene when they become aware of a wrongful or potentially dangerous situation. There are many factors (above just assessing the nature of the offense and whether it would be safe to intervene) that will determine whether or not a "bystander" will choose to step-up and engage in the prevention a potential harmful situation. Research has shown that arbitrary factors such as the potential victim's attractiveness, or the sex of the person being wronged, will impact a bystander's decision to act. More so, a bystander's decision to intervene will hinge greatly upon two factors: whether or not they feel a responsibility to act, and whether or not they feel they are capable of acting.

Let's take a closer look at this. First of all, for the average student, employee, or citizen to feel a responsibility to act, we have to assume that they have a "community based" belief system by which they live. Most people aren't generally motivated to do something for someone else unless there is a specific benefit or reward for them. That should sound familiar, as it is closely related to the "WII F.M." principle.

In the case of bystander intervention, very rarely is there a specific benefit for the person intervening, other than for them to know that intervening is simply the "right thing to do." Banking on the belief that "most people will act because it is the right thing to do," is misguided. Research has shown that when there are several people aware of a bad situation or recognize that a person needs help, the LESS likely it is that they will intervene. Most of the time, it is because of the assumption that "it is someone else's problem," or that "someone else will take care of it."

By collectively mobilizing, engaging, and becoming intolerant of unacceptable behavior (no matter how small), we can prevent the escalation to more harmful and dangerous behaviors. Inappropriate behavior (think: disrespectful language, actions, bullying, predatory behavior) cannot survive in an environment that won't allow it. We need to create that environment, and we especially need to create that environment on college campuses so that it is a physically and emotionally safe place for everyone to learn, live, and work. The entire campus community plays a valuable role in preventing acts that harm the community or violate basic human dignity.

A lot of people have been asking me about "these new bystander intervention strategies." "What's the big deal? Why does this really matter to students anyway?" My direct response is that bystander intervention programming actually matters to everyone, and the concept of helping behavior is far from "new." It's easy to think of situations in which a person who is neither the perpetrator nor the victim observes an event and has the power to change the outcome for the better. What these "new" bystander intervention strategies offer are the tools for those observers to actually step in appropriately and safely.

For many people, the problem in understanding "bystander intervention" strategies lies with the word "bystander" itself. "Bystander" literally means someone who is standing by, a witness to, but not participating in. So trying to mobilize people who are "standing by" is a tough concept for people to wrap their heads around. For example, many people, regardless of their work context, witness social injustices such as racial slurs, passive aggressive workplace discrimination, or maybe even not-so-subtle forms of coercion. People who "witness" these things, or who are aware of these behaviors, usually choose not to get involved in stopping the problem by rationalizing that "it has nothing to do with me," "it's not my problem," or "someone else here will take care of it." This is known as the "bystander effect" and the "diffusion of responsibility."

The error in this type of thinking is that when people witness events, such as bullying, racism, or dating abuse, they are condoning the behavior they are witnessing. People assume that ignoring the problem, or acting like they didn't see the problem, will make it go away. The reality is that ignoring the problem does not make it go away, and just like a wound left unattended, the problem will actually grow and possibly become more dangerous. People also assume that since they are not engaging in the inappropriate behavior or are not a direct victim of the injustice, that "standing by" seems like the safest and most "neutral option." Doing nothing is never a neutral option.

Doing nothing tacitly empowers the perpetrator, and quite frankly, doing nothing is in essence making a choice in favor of the socially toxic behavior further facilitating the creation of an environment that allows it. *If you do nothing, nothing changes!*

The confusion surrounding bystander intervention goes beyond the word bystander. It also has to do with our understanding of the terms "victim" and "perpetrator." When we use the nouns victim and perpetrator, we rigidly isolate and categorize people, events, and behaviors. Nouns such as victim and perpetrator are emotionally charged and come with a whole slew of subjective interpretations of what it means to "be a victim" or to "be a perpetrator." Most of the time, this type of thinking allows us to rationalize and "write ourselves" out of the equation because we don't categorize or label ourselves as fitting into one of those categories.

With that being said, I challenge you to stop thinking about the cycle of violence as being relevant only to those who are direct victims and perpetrators. I encourage you to start looking at the problem from a different perspective. For example, stop using the nouns and start using the verbs. The term victim refers only to a small percentage of people; however, the number of those who have been "victimized" by the cycle of violence is much greater. I am not a victim of sexual violence, but I have absolutely been victimized by it every time I had to worry if my roommate would make it home ok, when a friend needed my support after being assaulted, and when my campus was profiled in the news as an unsafe place; I am not a victim of workplace bullying or harassment, but I have been victimized by it. I have witnessed how these things affect the lives of loved ones and coworkers, and as a friend, sibling, co-worker, supervisor, and most importantly as a leader, I realize that if I am not part of the solution, I could very well be part of the problem. If you embrace this line of thinking, you will understand why people make the choice to intervene when they see "things going badly." Make the choice to draw a line in the sand regarding the types of behavior you will allow in your presence, and lets all participate in creating a living, learning, and working environment that is socially healthy for everyone.

The Primary Reasons Why People Don't Intervene

There are many reasons why people choose not to intervene in a situation. Let's take a look at some of the more prominent ones.

First of all, people will assume the situation isn't a "problem" and fail to interpret the situation as needing help. If you utilize good risk assessment and threat assessment skills, and learn to identify red flag risk indicators, you will be well equipped to identify a situation as one requiring help.

Most people assume a situation isn't a "problem" because most situations of discrimination and bullying appear ambiguous. People are generally afraid to inquire if there is a problem for fear that they may be the only one that "feels that way" and don't want to risk being embarrassed if they are. However, statistics show that when one person steps up, intervenes, or inquires about an ambiguous situation or a potentially discriminatory remark, others are also thinking and feeling the same way.

Second, people assume the situation is "none of their business" and fail to take personal responsibility. Even when bystanders do recognize a problem, most believe that it isn't THEIR problem, and will choose to ignore it or act like they aren't aware of it. This is where empathy and perspective taking come into play. Bystanders must ask themselves, "What would I want someone to do for me if I were in this situation?" Usually, the answer to that question provides the bystander with the most appropriate course of action.

Third, people assume someone else will "do something." This is a dangerous assumption, and is related to a phenomenon known as the "diffusion of responsibility," whereby each bystander's sense of responsibility actually decreases as the number of potential witnesses increases. This simply means that most people assume someone else will surely help because other people are there.

Finally, people make the false assumption that other people aren't bothered by the problem, and feel they don't know how to safely intervene because they don't have the proper skills *to intervene*. As stated above, most people are bothered by discriminatory remarks and harassment, but most people lack the communication and social skills necessary to appropriately address the problem. In learning skills such as Beyond Active Listening, the Persuasion Sequence, Redirections, Engagement Phrases, and Emotion Guards, bystanders are better equipped to confidently defuse the situation through conversation. In providing risk assessment skills, assertiveness training, and communication skills, bystanders will have the skills they need to identify problems, mobilize their peer groups, and be prepared to better protect themselves and others.

Here's What You Can Do to Help: Bystander Intervention Strategies

Bystander intervention should be understood as a life skill. Bystanders who mobilize are known to positively change the outcome of all sorts of situations, including cases of bullying, harassment, and assault. People who intervene can also change the outcome for people who are struggling to get help for things like disordered eating and depression, as sometimes all it takes is for someone to pay attention and choose to show concern.

There is no right or wrong way to choose to intervene, and I am not encouraging you to intervene in a situation that you feel is beyond your ability. If you choose to intervene, do so only when you know you are capable of handling the situation, and you know that you won't make the situation worse.

However, there are many college bystander intervention programs out there, which teach you how to directly and indirectly intervene, in both emergency and non-emergency situations. Programs such as University of Arizona's Step UP! Program, the Marquette University

T.A.K.E.S. A.C.T.I.O.N. Program, and the Men Can Stop Rape Program are just a few. Below is a summary of the best bystander intervention strategies to come out of those programs.

Presence

Sometimes your presence alone is enough to deter a situation. Think about surveillance cameras in a room; people will generally alter their behavior because they know their being watched, and they know they could get caught. If you are known as a person who won't tolerate bullying or hazing, the likelihood of it occurring in your presence will decrease. Presence as a strategy is also useful because it allows you to "monitor" a situation from a safe distance. This way, if you're unsure if a situation requires help, you can observe it and take mental notes of what is going on, in case something does go wrong.

Group Intervention

There is safety and power in numbers. This strategy is best used with someone who has a clear pattern of inappropriate behavior where many examples can be presented as evidence of their problem. This strategy is designed to let others know that they are not alone in their discomfort. For example, you might simply turn to the group and ask, "Am I the only one uncomfortable with this?" This creates options by allowing you to evaluate the situation and recruit the help of friends to determine your best move.

Clarification

People who express negative attitudes towards people expect other people to go along with them, laugh, and join in. They do not expect to be questioned. By asking a question like, "I'm not really sure what you mean by that. Could you explain that to me?" you create the opportunity to either rethink the assumptions that underlie their statements and attitudes or to empower others to express their disagreement.

Bring It Home

This strategy is designed to give perspective to whomever is acting in a degrading manner. It "re-humanizes" their target and makes them think about what it would be like if someone was treating somebody they knew like that. For example, if someone makes fun of another student saying they're a "total loser" because they have Attention Deficit Disorder (ADD), you could simply say, "Whoa, time out. How you would you feel if you're brother had ADD? You wouldn't think he's such a loser then."

"I" Statements

Think about how you feel when someone points the finger at you, and someone says in an accusatory voice, "YOU really need to stop acting like that, you're embarrassing the family." Instead think about how "I" statements are easier to hear since they are about the feelings and thoughts of the person making the statement, and not criticizing and accusing the other person. People are less likely to become defensive when using "I" statements. For example, you could say, "I find it embarrassing when you act like that. I'd like it if you could change you behavior in the future."

Humor

Humor is a difficult strategy as it can easily escalate if people feel they're being mocked. However, if you use humor effectively, it can reduce the tension inherent in the interventions and make it easier for the person to hear you. Be careful, though, not to be so funny that you undermine the point you're trying to make.

Silent Stare

This strategy works very well if you connect it to parents, who have the ability to communicate displeasure simply by staring. No words even need to be spoken. Sometimes a disapproving look can be far more powerful than words. Think about a time someone you really respected just looked at you and shook their head in disapproval. Remember how awful you felt?

Distraction

The goal of this strategy is not to directly confront the situation, but rather to interrupt it so that you change the course of it. This is an especially useful technique where there is a higher risk of physical violence, like a fight in progress or when there are multiple actors and only one of you). Use a distraction to redirect the focus somewhere else, or to draw their attention away from their target.

"We're Friends, Right?"

This strategy works best if you can take your friend (or another person) off to the side or if you can wait until later to confront them. That way, you can avoid humiliating them and increase the likelihood that they will hear and value what you say. For example, if you overhear a friend say something awful about another friend, you can talk to them after the fact and say, "Hey, we're friends, right? I don't want to fight with you, but I didn't like what you said about Tom earlier."

Cut and Divide

Step in and separate the two people and recruit help to do this if need be. By separating the two people, you can help them "cool off" and you can avoid them trying to posture or escalate in front of their friends. Don't use this strategy where you'd face a high risk of physical injury.

Take a Picture

Have a camera phone? Use technology to your advantage. People immediately sensor their behavior when they know they are being recorded! It is now easier than ever to record good witness information for police. Notice a security camera? Politely point it out to the person who is acting up, and remind them that it's not worth getting caught.

Engagement Phrases

Now that you have a solid understanding of bystander intervention strategies, you're starting to see all of the options you have to help yourself and others if you hear something inappropriate or see something going badly. Most of the time, however, it won't be enough just to know what to do; you also have to know what to say. If you recall back to some of the communication strategies you learned about earlier, you will remember the "Redirections" that you can use to change the course of a confrontation. Like Redirections, "Engagement Phrases" are phrases you can use to quickly intervene and get the attention of the other person. Engagement Phrases should be short, quick, and just long enough to tactfully get your point across without escalating the situation. If you use an engagement phrase to get involved in a situation, just remember that you have to match your verbal and non-verbal cues to "sell" the statement. The phrase must be delivered both verbally and non-verbally as non-escalatory and non-judgmental.

Here are some examples:

- "This is 'X-school.' That is not what we are about."

- "I hope no one talks about you like that."

- "The team needs you and expects more from you."

- "You may not have offended me, but your words/actions/behaviors, may have offended someone else."

- "Could you please clarify what you just said? I'm not sure I understood that correctly."

- "I know you are better than that."

- "Wow, do you really feel that way about 'x' person/group/behavior?"

- "I didn't expect that from you."

- "We've always been able to work things out in the past."

- "Would you work with me here?"

- "This is good for you, good for me, and good for everybody/the team/ this school."

- "Please leave with me. I have a concern for our safety."

Bystander Intervention Tips

As a bystander witness, you don't have to intervene directly (such as talking with the person immediately). You can choose to indirectly intervene by speaking with another person who you feel could be helpful in addressing or resolving the issue after the fact (such as a friend, teacher, coach, administrator, counselor, etc.)

If you do recognize a problem and choose to respond, try and remember the following tips adapted from the 'University of Arizona's Step UP! Program' that utilizes Vistelar conflict management principles:

- Investigate an unclear event further, and/or ask others what they think of the situation.

- Know your limits as a helper—engage others as necessary.
  Ask yourself what could happen if you don't intervene, and

determine if there's someone else better equipped to help. Don't unnecessarily put yourself in danger! Quickly decide if the situation is a concern for safety, or a concern for life. This will help you determine if the situation is an emergency, or non-emergency.

- Be mindful of peer pressure and be prepared to respond to it. Not everybody intervenes; if they did, we wouldn't have to talk about bystander intervention. Some people may question why you're trying to help another person, or why you're going against the grain. Use it as an opportunity to set context for them and change their perspective.

- Conduct conversations in a safe environment. Maintain mutual respect and mutual purpose. Be mindful of the "greater than, less than, and equal to" concept, and reflect that in your tone. Try to develop the right atmosphere for positive communication so that you don't inadvertently come across as accusatory, which would result in a defensive reaction.

- Remember that how you say things is more important than what you say. When forming your intervention conversation, be mindful of: Who (you're speaking to, or who is all involved), What (the exact content of what you want to say—utilize Precision of Word Choice), When (how you time the delivery), Where (you have the conversation, consider the location and level of privacy), Why (the reason you are talking with them) and How (tone, pace, pitch, modulation, and non-verbal behavior).

- Consider the frequency, duration, and intensity or/severity of the behavior when evaluating a situation and determining the best way to talk about it. Does this behavior happen often? What is the result of the behavior? The answers to those questions will help you determine WHAT to say, HOW to say it, and WHEN you need to intervene.

- Be sensitive, understanding, and non-judgmental. Utilize Beyond Active Listening and an empathetic presentation style, both verbally and non-verbally.

- Determine the priority outcome goal. What is the behavior you are hoping to stop? And what is the behavior/outcome you are trying to encourage? With those answers, you can formulate a plan and prepare/practice what you want to say.

- Be creative! Interrupt/distract/delay a situation you think might be problematic—before it becomes an emergency!

Post-Action Aftermath

Whether you choose to intervene in a situation or not, you may find yourself in a position where you have to relay information to the authorities. Using the skills outlined in this book will undoubtedly make you a better witness and improve your ability to relay accurate information to the police. If you intervened in an emergency situation, such as a multiple injury car accident, you may find yourself a little "shook up" from being involved in something you've seen before.

After the incident, especially if you had to get physical, take a quick self-assessment. Are you physically OK? Check for injuries. Did you get hit in the head? Then you will most likely want to get checked out. Are you mentally OK? Take a few deep breaths, slow down your thinking, and drink a glass of water. Taking some time to process what happened is good psychological first aid, and it will help you relay accurate information to authorities. In addition to police and security, be prepared to explain what happened to your family and friends, as they will likely have questions and want to hear about what you did. You may have to explain all of the things you saw and heard that lead up to the event. Thinking all of those things through will help you understand and justify your "reactions" to what happened.

What About Self-Defense?

I couldn't write a book on campus safety and not acknowledge the need for self-defense training. As you've learned throughout the book, things could get physical at any time. If the "fight" comes to you, you need to be prepared to defend yourself. Take a minute to assess your physical fitness level and your overall physical ability. How much confidence do you have in your ability to defend yourself if your life suddenly depended on it? Some of you may have extensive self-defense and/or martial arts training, and some of you may have none at all. Even if you have some training, I encourage you to seek out additional training and learn new skills. You can never have enough training. Check to see if your campus police or campus security offers training. Many times, colleges will host self-defense classes with little or no cost to you. If you can't find a local class, please check out: http://vistelar.com/training-calendar/ to see a list of all the training opportunities we have in your area. Can't find a class close? Give us a call. We can bring the training to you or your school!

"The world is a dangerous place to live; not because of the people who are evil, but because of the people who don't do anything about it."

— Albert Einstein

Jill Weisensel

Chapter 7

Putting It All Together

Throughout the course of this book, you have learned many new concepts. With training and practice, you will learn how to use these skills to keep you and your friends safe. Now I'd like to take a look at some of the specific situations that you will likely encounter on a college campus so you can better understand how to start using these skills right away. Some of the scenarios you will likely encounter are roommate conflicts, party conflicts, hazing, sexual assault situations, spring break and study abroad conflicts, social media monitoring, school shooter situations/mass casualty incidents, and student-law enforcement interactions. Let's take a look.

Roommate Conflicts

Yes, it's true. Your roommate may not be exactly what you were hoping for. One of the primary sources of stress for college students, in addition to academics and the mounting pressure of student loan repayment, is not getting along with their roommates. In extreme cases, your university may be able to reassign you to a new room or provide you with a different roommate, but that isn't always the case.

That means that you will have to effectively communicate with them to manage conflict, or you run the risk of constantly fighting with them or trying to avoid them all year. That is not a situation you want to find yourself in, especially while trying to manage your class load and extracurricular activities.

If you do find yourself in a conflict with your roommate, be prepared to use the Persuasion Sequence, Emotion Guards, and Redirections to help you navigate the conversation. Remember all the way back to the beginning of the book when Jordan stole Amanda's iPod on the first day of school? Let's use some of these communication skills to try and get Amanda's iPod back:

Amanda: "Jordan? I can't find my iPod. Have you seen it?"

Jordan: "Nope."

Amanda: "Really? Because I left it right here charging before I left and you were the only one in the room. It's important to me—my dad bought it for my birthday. Are you sure you haven't seen it?" (ask and explain why)

Jordan: "No. Sorry."

Amanda: "Ok Jordan, well here's the thing. I left it here and I was only gone an hour. You were the only one in the room. If you took it, I don't really care about the cops at this point—I just want it back. So here are the options. I will leave the room and go to dinner. If you took it, please put it back on my desk. No questions asked and I won't speak of it again. But if I leave and you don't put it back, I'm going to have to talk with hall staff and possibly even the campus police. You and I are both trying to study abroad next year; you know we don't need to have our names in a police report which would jeopardize our chances of getting into the program. Could you work with me here?" (offer options, let them choose)

Jordan: "Oh, I didn't know that a police report could hurt our chances of going abroad. Well. Ok. I guess I will see you after dinner then."

As you can see, the progression of the Persuasion Sequence helped Amanda steer the conversation towards a positive outcome. In this situation, Amanda would have most likely gone to dinner and found her iPod on her desk when she got back. And if not? Well then Amanda would confirmed Jordan's non-cooperation (give opportunity to reconsider) and, possibly, would need to Take Appropriate Action by talking with hall staff. Let's take a look at another situation using a room party example. This time Jordan will be even more verbally resistant to Amanda's request:

Amanda: "Dude, Jordan, it's Wednesday night and you've got like six people in the room drinking, and you're music is pretty awful. Could you please move the party somewhere else?" (Step One)

Jordan: "Hey Amanda what's up??! You should just stop talking and come pre-game with us. That sounds like a better idea!"

Amanda: "Jordan seriously, it's a Wednesday night, we both have an exam tomorrow at 8 a.m., and I really need to study. Could you please go somewhere else?" (ask and explain why)

Jordan: "No way, this is my room too. I'm already failing the class. So how about you take your brainiac self down to the library."

Amanda: "Well I'm sorry you're failing, but we could turn that around you know (Redirection). I could help you. But right now I am asking you to please be respectful of our space. I think we have some good options here. Brooke's roommate is one and no one is over there. Why don't you go party over there where you can have louder music and less hall staff walk through. I'd hate to see you guys get caught for drinking in the dorm." (offer options, let them choose)

Jordan: "Ha, we'll never get caught."

Amanda: "Look. I don't want to see you get written up again. Anyone on this floor could call you in right now. Don't risk it. Is there anything I can say to get you to move this party?" (give opportunity to reconsider)

Jordan: "Um. No."

Amanda: "Alright then, I'm sorry. I'm going to have to talk with hall staff."

I've seen the Persuasion Sequence resolve hundreds of conflicts, with a positive result and nobody getting hurt. Aside from being able to communicate with your roommate, here are a couple other tips that you should be mindful of regarding your room, especially if you're living in a community style dormitory or residence hall:

• Don't ever leave your door unlocked or promote an "always open, come on in" policy. Lock your door, even if you leave "just for a minute."

• Don't leave notes on your door or your door's dry erase board saying where you are or when you'll be back. This is just telling everyone that your room is unoccupied. Send a text or call your friends that need to know where you are.

• If you have card or key access to your building, be mindful of people "piggy backing" your entry in order to gain access. If you don't recognize them, don't hesitate to ask them if they have their key, or what they're doing in the building. If you are too shy to talk to them, try and monitor where they go in the building so you can relay the information to hall staff. The person may have access to the building, but they may not. It is best to clarify.

- If you have prescription drugs, keep them in the prescription containers and keep them in a secure place. Prescription drug theft is increasing on college campuses, and there are hefty fines and jail time associated with being in possession of unmarked prescription medication!

Party Conflicts and Hazing

Partying is an undeniable truth of campus life, and yes, some students party a whole lot more than others. The belief that every student parties and the belief that every student drinks is a myth. In fact, research shows that over 70% of incoming college students identify as alcohol abstainers before they get to college. However, there are certain aspects of college life, such as unstructured time, the widespread availability and promotion of alcohol, and limited interactions with parents or other adults, which can increase the number of students who participate in high risk drinking behaviors, such as binge drinking and pre-gaming.

With that being said, you will most likely find yourself either facing some type of party related conflict during your college career. It could be noise complaints from loud music, medical incidents as a result of intoxication, or intoxicated friends damaging property or getting into fights. And believe it or not, contrary to popular belief, alcohol is also considered the number one date rape drug. Alcohol is involved in over 80% of campus sexual assaults. Regardless of what extent you choose to participate in the "college party scene," the impact of alcohol and alcohol-induced behavior will inevitably be all around you.

Dealing with intoxicated friends can be extremely frustrating. You will find yourself trying to talk with them and pleading with them to go home, and they will fight you. They will yell at you and call you names. They will be wasted and they will tell you that they still don't want to leave. They could also get angry and physically aggressive with you—I've heard many stories of college students taking swings at and actually punching their friends while intoxicated.

This is the arena where you will want to be on your "A" game, and you will put all of your skills to the test. In the 540 Degree Proxemic Management section, we talked about being mindful of your hands—to keep them above waist height in case you need to quickly protect your face. Well, this is where it becomes a reality. Imagine trying to help an intoxicated friend who has fallen to the ground, and as you lean over to put your arm around them and pick them up, they try to push you away and accidently punch you in the face. It does happen, and noses are broken, and teeth are knocked out. Don't get complacent just because they are your friends; use the skills you have learned!

The last time we left Jordan, she was debating about what to do when Amanda was faced with having to do a keg stand that she didn't want to do. Let's take a look at what happened next:

Jordan looked at Amanda and knew she had to intervene. "Boys, boys, boys," she said, "Don't waste beer on someone who doesn't want to drink. I will gladly help you out." Brian laughed, "Aw come on, I already know you like to drink. Come help us." "Actually, I'm pretty sure she will just get sick and throw up on your new Air Maxes. Besides, I don't want to be responsible for her the rest of the night. Why don't you guys just stop?" As Jordan was deciding her options, Amanda's friend Brooke stopped in the kitchen and overheard Jordan's objection. "Oh hey girl, we've been looking for you! You're coming with me." Brooke and Jordan then grabbed Amanda, and took her out of the house. "Thanks guys," Amanda said. "No problem," Brooke replied, "It was time to get out of there anyway. Let's go get something to eat."

As you can see, it was a combination of Jordan's communication skills and Brooke's level of awareness and quick intervention strategy (Cut and Divide) that helped get Amanda out of the negative situation. The more scenarios you encounter, the easier it will become for you to put all of the intervention pieces together. Pretty soon, it will just become second nature.

There is, however, another dangerous activity that goes hand in hand with college parties, and that's hazing. Hazing is an extreme form of "initiating" someone into a new group, whether it be a new group of friends, a team, club, or organization. The initiation process often involves drinking or being forced to drink an excessive amount of alcohol, and participation in an activity or series of activities that are embarrassing or demeaning to the initiate. If you find yourself in a hazing situation, or you become aware of a hazing situation before, during, or after the fact, you must realize the seriousness of the issue. While you may have the skills you need to directly intervene in a hazing situation, you must consider the fact that hazing is group driven and ritualistic, and if you try to intervene directly, you will most likely face an extreme amount of peer pressure and disapproval.

If you become aware of a hazing incident, get as much information as you can about it: when and where it is occurring (or has occurred), who is all involved, and what types of activities will be taking place. Take this information to campus authorities immediately. This will be one of those situations where you may fear that you are "snitching" and won't want to get involved. However, there is a difference between snitching, or tattling to maliciously get someone in trouble, and reporting, which is trying to prevent a situation from getting worse. Extreme incidents of hazing have contributed to many student injuries and deaths. Report the information that is necessary, and you may just save the life of one of your friends.

Finally, if you do decide to party and you do decide to drink, remember these tips:

- Drink only if you are of legal age to drink, and drink in moderation.

- Know your limits. This means being mindful of the effects of "a beer," versus "several beers," and knowing how different drinks affect you. College parties often involve drinking games, where you could potentially be drinking a large quantity of alcohol in a short amount of time. This is a sure fire way to get yourself extremely sick. Remember, the danger of drinking goes beyond just the medical danger. Drinking is dangerous because of what actions and behaviors take place while intoxicated.

- Be conscious of what is "a drink," and understand different cup sizes.

- Watch your drink. Never accept alcohol from people you don't know, and if you leave your drink unattended for any period of time, dump it out and get a new one.

- Go out in a group. If you leave with friends, make sure you come back with them. Before you go out, determine what time you will plan on leaving, and designate a driver. If you aren't driving, it is still a good idea to designate a sober watchdog for your group.

- Take only what you really need with you. Do you really need everything that is in your wallet or purse? Just bring the amount of money you need, your ID, and your phone. I can't tell you how many people I know who have gone out thinking they'd only spend $50 in a night, only to find out the next day (sober) that they picked up a $300 bar tab on their credit card.

Party Conflicts and Sexual Assault

Parties also serve as a place to meet new people and to hang out with new friends. You may even meet somebody that you'd like to get into a relationship with. Some of your parents may have even been college sweethearts. But there is also a dark side to the world of college parties and campus life, and that includes dating violence and sexual assaults. This may be a very difficult topic for some of you to read about, as many people have already been directly affected by this type of crime. If you find this topic too difficult for you, please take care of yourself, and if you need to skip to the next section—please do!

Sexual assault may be uncomfortable to think about, and you may even be thinking, "It will never happen to me." But, the sad truth is that it does happen, and it happens way more than it should on college campuses all over the country. In fact, statistics show that each year, an estimated 97,000 students (between the ages of 18 and 24) are victims of alcohol related sexual assault. It is estimated that 1 in 5 women (that's 20%) will be the victim of sexual assault during her time at college, and they are the most vulnerable to sexual assault during the first few weeks at school (think: new environment, peer pressure to drink, meet new people, and fit in). But sexual assault is not just a woman's issue—men are also the victims of sexual assault. If you've had any previous sexual assault prevention training, I'm sure you've heard something like, "If you're a female, protect yourself so you don't get raped." The advice to protect yourself is just as important for men. Whether you are a male or a female, there are ways to increase your awareness to conditions that may make you (and your friends) more vulnerable, and precautions you can take to reduce your own vulnerability. And whether you're male or female, you need to understand the laws regarding consent so that if you engage in sexual activity you don't make assumptions about consent that are not what the other person wants, and fit the definition of sexual assault. It is important to remember that if you want a higher level of contact, you are responsible for understanding whether or not your partner is also interested in this level of sexual contact, and also knowing whether or not your partner is even able to give consent. These are critical points for you to understand, as the repercussions of sexual assault are devastating and lifelong for everyone involved. Because consent is so important, we will focus on it more in a little bit.

Before we do that, let's try and unpack this problem a little further and start with some overall context. First of all, in order to understand what dating violence and sexual assault are, we need to know what a healthy relationship actually looks like. Now I know you're thinking, "Duh, Jill, I'm in a good relationship; I know what it is." But it's worth being clear about what we mean when we talk about healthy (and unhealthy) relationships. So here are some traits of healthy relationships:

- Both parties are mutually invested in the relationship and in the enjoyment of each other.

- Both parties support each other's opportunities for growth.

- Both parties share their emotions.

- Non-sexual and sexual contact is intended to be mutually pleasing, and should build feelings of intimacy and trust.

So, as you can see, healthy relationships are mutual, respectful, and involve open communication. Unhealthy relationships include the opposite of the above list - they lack mutuality, respect and open communication. There are also several red flag risk indicators that are found amongst perpetrators of dating violence. They are:

- Quick attachment: you've only known each other for a short while, but suddenly their head over heels in love and already talking marriage and babies.

- Controlling behavior: they will try to prevent you from doing things you want to do, especially if you want to go without them. They will do things to manipulate your time.

- Jealousy: they become jealous of your other friends, hobbies, or successes.

- Blaming: they will continually blame you for things that were out of your control.

- "Hot" and "cold" behavior: they are generally quick to anger.

- These types of people will also try to belittle, intimidate, and humiliate you.

- They may also show signs of "stalking" behavior; things like showing up unexpectedly wherever you are, making direct threats, or sending cryptic or awkward e-mails, voicemails, or social media messages. If a situation reaches this level and you feel like you are being stalked, you probably are. Recognize the seriousness of the issue- if the nature of the behavior keeps escalating, cease contact and contact campus security/police.

Now that you get the general idea of what distinguishes a healthy relationship from an unhealthy one, let's take a look at sexual assault and what leads up to it.

Sexual assault can be committed by someone you're dating, by someone you don't even know, or by someone you hardly know. On college campuses, over 90% of sexual assaults are committed by persons known to the victim—meaning they either knew them from a class, a party, or through friends. In your mind, I'm sure you're thinking that this sounds like it could be "date rape." I am choosing not to use the term date rape because it undermines the seriousness of sexual assault. If a sexual assault reaches the level of rape, it is in fact rape. Different states have different laws and classifications for sexual assault, so you should talk with your campus security/police and ask them about the sexual assault laws and statutes that pertain to your particular campus. For the purpose of this book, however, I am going to use an umbrella classification for sexual assault, and define sexual assault as "any unwanted contact that is sexual in nature."

Consent

You, and only you, can give consent to someone else to touch your body. Your body and your space are yours and yours alone. Remember earlier when Amanda was being dragged to the keg? While that is not an example of sexual contact, it is an example of non-consensual contact- the other students did not have permission to grab her, because Amanda never consented and said they could.

With that being said, I am not going to talk about the moral ramifications of engaging in sexual behaviors. I am simply acknowledging that at some point, college students will face a decision to engage in sexual activity, and unfortunately, many of you will find yourselves in a position where someone is trying to pressure you into engaging in some type of sexual activity.

If you find yourself being pressured into doing something you don't want to do—don't do it! Any pressure to engage in any type of behavior is a red flag risk indicator, also called "aggressor characteristics." This is just one of many red flag risk indicators that have been found amongst perpetrators of sexual assault. According to the Student Success "Unless There's Consent" sexual assault prevention education program and nationally recognized clinical psychologist and sexual assault prevention consultant, Dr. David Lisak, examples of red flags indicators include:

- The perpetrator has a strong belief in traditional gender roles.

- They are selfish about the relationship, or about their time
  with you.

- They typically have a strong male social group.

- They lack respect for personal boundaries. People who don't respect your personal space, touch you inappropriately, or pursue affection early in a relationship are at greater risk of being predators.

- They have "rape myth" acceptance: they think that the victim of rape "had it coming" because of the way they dressed, where they were walking, etc.

- They are poor communicators, generally manipulative, and full of excuses.

- They have trust issues. People who raise trust issues early in a relationship, saying things like "don't you trust me?" are at very high risk for predatory behavior. Such statements are often a sign that they don't actually trust themselves. Trust is something that develops slowly in a relationship and is earned with time and experience. There is no reason to fully trust someone you don't know well.

- They "push" drugs or alcohol on their victims (over 80% of campus sexual assaults involve alcohol because alcohol limits inhibitions and slows our decision making ability). Someone who pushes you to use drugs or alcohol is high risk. It is important to question someone's motives when they seem set on getting you drunk.

- They are violent or have a history of violence (towards other people, animals, or property for example).

Remember, just because someone may exhibit red flag behaviors, it doesn't mean they are "a rapist." Research has shown that that majority of sexual predators are men, but that over 94% of men will never commit this crime. Of the 6% who do, many are repeat offenders. So with that being said, people exhibiting one or two of these traits aren't necessarily sexual predators, but someone exhibiting many of these red flags, may be. Pay attention to the red flags and take inventory of them in an effort to protect yourself and others.

Finally, you should educate yourself about consent. As I mentioned earlier, only you can give consent to someone else to touch your body. Again, different states legally define consent in different ways, so you should check with your campus authorities to determine the legal way in which consent is defined on your campus. However, I can provide you with some general guidelines. Generally speaking, if alcohol is involved in any way, you are treading in dangerous territory because most laws surrounding consent include a clause that if you're intoxicated, you can't legally give consent. Remember, there's a reason why over 80% of college sexual assaults involve alcohol. Additionally, the burden of getting consent falls to whichever person is trying to elevate to the next level of intimacy. Consent must be freely given to that person, and the process of giving and getting consent should be continuous. Consent should be a clearly defined, clearly stated, and enthusiastically stated "yes." Consent is *not* the absence of "no." And lastly, if you remember nothing else about consent, remember that if "fear is in the room, consent is not." If you fear for your safety or feel pressured or coerced in any way to engage in any type of sexual activity, don't do it. Communicate clearly that you are uncomfortable with the situation, and if you need to, leave and/or get help.

A Word about High Stress Situations and Trauma

Over 80% of the time, a victim of sexual assault will disclose to a friend that they've been assaulted before they will report it to campus authorities. In the event that someone discloses to you that they've been sexually assaulted, it is imperative that you believe them. Sexual assault is a highly traumatic experience, and the information they are telling you may seem confusing to you, and that's OK. Just listen, and be there for them. Encourage them to report the crime to the police (if and when they are ready to). If the sexual assault just occurred, encourage them not to change their clothes, not to wash their clothes, not to shower, and encourage them to go to a local sexual assault treatment center. This will be difficult for both you and your friend, but with strength and support, you can help them through this horrible experience.

There are many reasons why victims of sexual assaults are scared to report the crime to the police. They are generally scared that no one will believe them, for one, and they are generally humiliated and embarrassed. Sexual assault victims may also experience a lot of self-blaming and self-shaming, and struggle to grasp the idea that they could possibly be a "rape victim." In the event that they knew their attacker, it is also difficult for them to believe that someone they trusted could be a "rapist." As they are struggling to make sense of this situation, again, it is crucial that you believe them and offer your support.

As a result of the trauma, it could be difficult for them to recall the exact specifics of the event. Facts may seem missing, and the chronology of what lead up to the assault may seem disjointed. This is in fact, a completely normal response amongst individuals who have experienced a traumatic event. After a high stress incident, whereas their "fight or flight" instincts may have kicked in, it could actually take someone two full sleep cycles before actually being able to recall events surrounding the incident. Be mindful of this fact, and be the best ally to the sexual assault survivor you can be!

Spring Break

Spring break stories are legendary. I'm sure you've all heard the crazy spring break stories, filled with sun and beach time. When you finally decide where you're going for spring break, you're going to need to do a safety assessment before you leave, as it will be a new environment for you.

Here are some tips:

- Find out if your spring break spot is in a high crime neighborhood, and get the phone number for local police.

- Tell your family (or someone you trust back home) exactly where you will be staying, when you will be leaving, and when you'll be home.

- Find out if your hotel has camera systems and controlled entry.

- Determine the safest route to get to the beach and night life.

- Locate the closest hospital.

- When you travel, always keep your belongings close to you.

- If you need to use local transportation, use a real cab line, or be sure to validate freelance sources.

Study Abroad

If you choose to study abroad, you will be faced with the challenge of learning yet another new environment. It is important that you learn all that you can about where you will be living, before you get there. Talk to students who have studied where you're going, and to people who have lived in the same place that you will be living. If you don't know anyone, talk with your study abroad coordinator so that you can get specific information about the area. Here are some tips regarding information you should be gathering:

- Find out if it's in a high crime neighborhood, and get the phone number for local police.

- Find out if your new residence has camera systems and controlled entry.

- Determine the safest route to get to your classes.

- Locate the closest hospital.

- Program the emergency contact numbers for your school in case you need them.

Social Media: The Era of the Digital Tattoo

In the era of social media and digital everything, now more than ever, our personal information is everywhere. If you think I'm kidding, run a search engine search of your name and find out just how many things the internet knows about you—maybe even things you wish it didn't. While you're away at college, it may be tempting to put a lot of your contact information online, but don't give into the temptation. Putting your personal information online will only set you up for trouble, including potential stalking incidents and identity theft. You have a lot more to lose than you do to gain from putting highly personal information online. Identity theft comes in many forms. People can steal your personal information through:

- Social media sites

- Phishing and Pharming

- "Dumpster Diving"

- "Shoulder Surfing"

Limit the amount of personal information you upload to your social media sites. It's OK to be vague. Try using a city nickname or come up with a creative job title. Everything you upload to the internet will forever become your digital tattoo. If using social media sites such as Facebook or Foursquare, consider using a name other than your real name, and think twice about where and when you "check in" to locations. Yes, checking in is a cool way to tell your friends where you are, but it also alerts people you don't want following you of your location. Use common sense so that people can't track your every move. Additionally, be mindful of the types of pictures you post, as employers are increasingly surveying the social media sources of potential hires!

Phishing and pharming are two additional ways in which people try to steal your information, either through e-mail or through actual legitimate websites, such as sites you may buy products from. If you choose to make online purchases, make sure you are buying from reputable sellers that secure your banking information, and be careful of people who may be "shoulder surfing," looking over your shoulder, as you as you enter in personal information such as credit card numbers at computer kiosks or retrieve money from an ATM.

Dumpster diving is a method that people use to steal your personal information that literally involves them going through dumpsters or garbage cans to try and retrieve your personal information off of things like letters or credit card statements. Be sure to shred all of your mail or any other documents containing personal information that you no longer need.

Throughout the course of this book, I have mentioned several times how important it is to put away your cell phones and to look where you're going. Believe me; I love to text as much as the next person, so I know how hard this can be to do. However, it is possible to use your cell phone as a safety tool. Make sure it's fully charged before you head out, so that you don't run the risk of having a dead cell phone when you need someone's number or you need to look up GPS directions. Make a plan before you go out just in case your phone dies, so that you can meet up with your friends at a specific location at a predetermined time. If you find yourself in an uncomfortable situation, you can always use your phone to shoot a quick text to a friend so they can come pick you up.

Finally, it is believed that by 2016, over 90% percent of college students will have a smartphone. While you will probably utilize your smartphones for texting and surfing the web, there are several companies producing safety related smartphone applications. Smartphone apps are a great tool for students because they are easily accessible and typically low cost or free. These apps, such as Circle of 6 or Guardly, will allow you to alert certain people of your GPS location if you encounter a dangerous situation. These types of apps can also provide real-time emergency incident monitoring and communication with local authorities. Take a look at the applications available to, or speak with your campus authorities to see if they have any apps they recommend.

School Shooter and Mass Casualty Incidents

You have probably noticed the increase in school shootings over the past several years. You may even have experienced one close to your hometown, or worse, you may have lived through one. Regardless of your experience or level of knowledge surrounding school shooter incidents, there are many things that you can do to help keep yourself alive in the event that a shooting happens on your campus. Remember that we're practicing "when-then" thinking: although I hope you never have to use this information, I want you to be prepared in case you find yourself in such a crisis. The increase in school shootings has lead people to try and figure out the "profile" of a school shooter. Unfortunately, there is no "tried and true" profile of a person who will commit a school shooting. Research has shown that people do not typically just "snap," but will generally display indicators of potentially violent behavior over time. The Department of Homeland Security (DHS) advises that "if these behaviors are recognized early, they can often be managed." Potentially violent behaviors by a student may include one or more of the following (this list of behaviors produced by the DHS is not comprehensive, nor is it intended as a mechanism for diagnosing violent tendencies):

- Increased use of alcohol and/or illegal drugs

- Noticeable decrease in attention to appearance and hygiene

- Depression/withdrawal

- Resistance and overreaction to changes in policy and procedures

- Repeated violations of company policies

- Increased severe mood swings

- Noticeably unstable, emotional responses

- Explosive outbursts of anger or rage without provocation

- Suicidal comments

- Behavior which is suspect of paranoia. The "everybody is against me" mentality.

- Talk of previous incidents of violence

- Empathy towards individuals committing violent acts

If you observe somebody exhibiting a combination of these behaviors, it would be advisable to report the behavior to campus authorities. People exhibiting these behaviors may seem distressed, and you may start to hear subtle comments or verbal threats. Studies have shown that in many cases, persons who commit violent acts told someone else they were going to do it before the incident occurred. Threats can be made in person directly, or can be overheard. Threats can be:

Specific: "Just wait until everyone sees the bomb I've made.

They won't think I'm such a loser then."

Veiled: "I'd not show up to class tomorrow. Mr. Jones is going to get it."

Direct: "Don't talk down to me like that. I will make your life a living hell."

Indirect: "I just wish I'd never been born."

Conditional: "If he doesn't show up with my money, I will make him pay."

If you become aware of a threat, take it seriously and inform campus authorities. Even if the person was not serious, he or she may need help dealing with personal issues or stressors, and the campus personnel can help find the resources that person needs. Take good notes about their description, and take a picture of them if you can. This will help campus police locate the subject they may not recognize.

When the Shooting Starts

In the event that you are in class or on campus and you do hear gunfire, here is what to expect when the shooting starts.

Your body will most likely kick into a "fight or flight response." There are multiple physiological changes your body will experience during a "fight or flight adrenaline dump." You will experience perceptual narrowing (tunnel vision), near sightedness, auditory exclusion (extremely limited hearing), and a possible change in your perception of time. You will also experience a rapid increase in your heart rate and breathing, so it will be critical for you to control and slow your breathing to try and reverse these effects. You may also find that you are less receptive to communication, less capable of critical thinking or problem solving, and experience a loss of tactile function (shaking).

You will encounter chaos and confusion. You will need to recognize the sound of gunshots, and if you've never heard them in real life before, you will realize they sound much different than those in movies or video games. You will most likely witness many people trying to evacuate in a chaotic pattern.

In the event that you do hear gunfire, or you become aware of a school shooter on campus, either through your university's text messaging system or from a friend, you should first try to evacuate and get as far away from the shooter as possible. If you can get to an escape route, you should leave your belongings behind, and helps others escape if possible. According to the DHS, you should evacuate regardless of whether others agree to follow you, and you should do your best to prevent other people from entering an area where the active shooter may be. While you are escaping to safety, keep your hands visible (raised, empty, and fingers spread) so that incoming law enforcement officers can recognize that you are not a threat. Do not make any sudden movements towards them, or attempt to hold on to them for safety. Remain calm, and follow any instructions given to you by law enforcement officers. Do not stop or slow down to help move wounded people. Call 911 as soon as it is safe to do so, and if you have an accurate description of the shooter's identity or location, give it to them. A good example would include:

- Location of the active shooter

- Number of shooters, if more than one

- Physical description of shooter/s (height, weight, shape, clothing colors)

- Number and type of weapons held by the shooter/s (hand gun, rifle, shotgun etc.)

- Number of potential victims at the location

If you are unable to evacuate, it is advised that you try and hide. You need to locate a place where the active shooter is unlikely to find you. This should be a place out of the shooter's view, and should provide protection in the event that shots are fired in your direction. Don't go to place that traps or restricts your options for movement, and if you are behind a door, lock it and barricade it with heavy items. Be mindful to silence your phones, and try your best to remain silent, so as not to give away your location.

As a last resort, and only when your life is in imminent danger, attempt to disrupt and/or incapacitate the active shooter by acting as aggressively as possible against the shooter, by throwing items and improvising weapons. If you do choose to engage the shooter, you must commit to your actions, and realize it's a life or death situation.

"By failing to prepare, you are preparing to fail."
– Benjamin Franklin

Chapter 8

Uh oh, Cops!

"I'm so glad I didn't have to do that keg stand. Thank you for stepping in and intervening," Amanda said to a new friend. "You're welcome, it was the right thing to do. You looked really nervous," said Joanna, "I'm glad I could help. Do you want to sit outside and get some fresh air?" Amanda and Joanna left the party and decided to hangout on the front porch of the house. There were dozens of students outside, some were drinking alcohol, but many were just playing games and listening to music. Amanda looked around, took it all in, and smiled. "I really do love this campus," she said. Then, seemingly out of nowhere, three police cars pulled up and surrounded the house.

Amanda was struggling to see through the red and blue lights, but she saw several students throwing their cups and running from the house. She even saw a couple students getting chased by the police. Amanda was scared. She hadn't been drinking, but many underage students were. She wanted to run too, but she knew she hadn't done anything wrong. "Joanna, should we run?" The second she asked the question she regretted it. She was suddenly face to face with a police officer. "Excuse me miss. I'm Officer Thompson with the campus police. I'd like to ask you some questions about this party. Can I please see your driver's license?" Amanda froze. She had no idea what to do.

There may come a time during your college experience where you will find yourself speaking with law enforcement. Hopefully, it will be because your superior personal awareness skills allowed you to call in a crime that you witnessed. Unfortunately, you may find yourself the victim of a crime and needing to report critical information that could help lead to an arrest. In either case, you will need to know how to be a "good witness" by obtaining the most accurate information possible for the police. Here are some tips about how to be a better witness:

• Take deep breaths, and stay calm.

• Gather as much information about the situation as you can. If you see subject(s), identify their: name (if known), race, sex, type and color of clothing, body size, hair color, any distinguishing features such as jewelry, tattoos, scars, a distinctive smell, and the last known direction of travel.

• If you see a vehicle, try to identify the: make, model, color, number of doors, license plate, any distinguishing dents or rust spots, and the last known direction of travel.

• If you see a weapon, do the best you can to determine what type. Was it a knife or club? How long was it? If it was a gun, was it a handgun, rifle, or shotgun?

• If you come across something that looks suspicious, don't wait to call it in—response time is crucial for law enforcement.

• If you come across an emergency situation with multiple potential injuries, try to identify the number of people injured, their ages, and the extent of their injuries. Are they conscious and breathing? Do they have any gross deformities, or are they bleeding profusely?

Now, it is also possible that at some point you could find yourself in "trouble" with the police. College students usually experience "negative" contacts with law enforcement for actions like:

- Underage drinking/serving a minor/public drinking

- Fighting/disorderly conduct/battery or assault

- Indecent exposure/public urination

- Burglary

- Theft

- Vandalism

- Harassment

- Sexual assault

Recognize that these activities are against the law, and if you are found guilty of perpetrating in any of these activities, they come with heavy fines (anywhere from hundreds of dollars to thousands of dollars!) and possible jail time. So, in the event that you do find yourself interacting with law enforcement as a potential subject of a crime, here are some guidelines for making that interaction as positive as possible, which trust me, is absolutely in your best interest:

- Take deep breaths, and stay calm.

- Keep your hands out of your pockets and make no sudden movements.

- Be polite and respectful—comply with whatever the officer asks you to do.

- Be honest. Do not. Do NOT. Lie.

- Do not try to "butt in" and "be a hero" by defending a friend who got in trouble. If you remain respectful to the officers, they will remain respectful to you.

A citizen/law enforcement interaction is generally emotionally charged. If you find yourself being questioned regarding a crime, it will be important to use skills like Showtime Mindset and Emotion Guards and not get overly defensive. Just because an officer has stopped to talk to you doesn't mean that you necessarily "did something wrong." Law enforcement officers have tons of different reasons for why they stop and talk to people, and contrary to popular belief, the reasons aren't always bad!

On a college campus, you will most likely start to recognize many of the campus police and security officers during your first year of school. These officers won't be like the police officers you encounter off campus, because you will be seeing them and interacting with them over the course of a few years, not just for a brief moment in your life, like during a traffic stop for a speeding violation. And since you will be interacting with them for a few years, I highly encourage you to try and develop the best relationship possible with them. Campus safety professionals are everyday heroes, but behind the badges, they are just everyday normal people trying to help you stay safe. Vistelar Consultant and law enforcement officer Bill Singleton has conducted a substantial amount of work researching police and youth interactions. He has spent a good part of his career developing programs that help foster understanding and collaboration between students and law enforcement professionals because he knows just how critically important this relationship is to creating a safe environment for everyone. Being an expert on this topic, I asked Bill to write a guest chapter for this book to reiterate these skills and highlight his experience to help you understand the role you play in creating a safe campus environment that everyone can enjoy.

The Moment of Truth
By Bill Singleton

It was a normal September night. Some students were getting settled into their dorms, while others were venturing out to the party scene. It was my third year as a police officer on a college campus.

On this night I was assigned undercover, plainclothes duty. My assignment: underage alcohol consumption prevention. I was to try and detect underage alcohol possession before it led to consumption. Previously, I had worked three years as an undercover narcotics investigator for a different jurisdiction so this assignment seemed rather low key. I was walking with my partner near a well-known intersection when a group of students approached us. They were laughing, yelling and talking loud. More importantly, the majority of the students all had red solo-cups., which likely filled with some type of alcohol. My job that night was to stop them, make sure they were 21, and to educate them on the dangers of binge drinking and college parties. As the group approached, I pulled out my police-issued badge (which I was wearing around my neck) and identified myself as a police officer. The 9 students in the group froze. I asked them if anybody was 21. There was silence. I asked them for the ID's. Again, nobody moved. I told them that we needed to see their ID's.

As the students began giving us their ID's, a male student about 5' 9", 140 lbs., looked at me and said, "My friend has my wallet." I asked him where his friend was and he turned and yelled in a different direction. As he yelled, I made the mistake of turning away from him and looking. When I looked back, he was gone.

The chase was on. He was running so fast that there was no way I was going to catch him. He probably ran about 500 yards before I lost him. I had no idea where he had gone, but I knew he was in the area. We looked and looked for him. After about 45 minutes of looking, he popped up out the bushes (about 15 yards from me) and began running. Little did he know that he was running right into the path of my partner.

My partner (who was also in plainclothes) went to apprehend him, but missed. My partner's department-issued firearm fell to the ground sliding on the concrete. By the time I reached my partner, he was fighting with the student on the ground and his gun lay exposed to all the students walking by.

After a brief struggle, we were able to secure the student in handcuffs. I was able to secure my partner's firearm and nobody was seriously hurt.

Good ending for all? Not so fast. It turns out that the student who ran from us, fought with us, and was eventually placed into custody was a star soccer player on the University's team. He was charged with battery to a police officer, fleeing from a police officer, and underage alcohol possession. His parents, his coach, my partner and I, along with the students and the district attorney, met at the District Attorney's office to discuss the incident.

During the discussion, the district attorney asked the student why he didn't cooperate right away. The student said, "Because I didn't know what was going to happen. I have never had any contact with the police. I didn't know what to do." Because the student didn't know what to do, he panicked. That panic caused him a suspension from the team and academic probation along with 500 hours of community service. He lost his scholarship. Why? Did it have to happen? Could it have been prevented?

The answer is YES! For the last 17 years, I have been a police officer in the State of Wisconsin. I have worked undercover, patrol, community prosecution and in the Officer of Community Outreach & Education. In this last role, my job was to educate the public as to what it is police do, why we do it, where we do it, and how we do it.

My goal was for the public to have a better understanding of who we are so that if they are ever stopped, we can have a conversation rather than the situation I just described.

I'm very honored that Jill asked me to write a chapter in her book about "Police/Citizen Encounters." I've been fortunate to have had the opportunity to be one of the creators of an International Association Chiefs of Police award winning program entitled "Students Talking it Over with Police (STOP)" program. Chief Edward Flynn of Milwaukee Police Department came up with this great idea and trusted myself and my partner, Cullin Weiskopf, to create and develop a program that would address the relationship that exists between police and youth with the purpose of decreasing an initial hostile interaction. I have personally delivered presentations to over 2000 students and adults on the topic of police-citizen encounters, and have been on the advisory board for police-youth encounters for the Center of Court Innovation in New York City. In addition, I won The Milwaukee Business Journals' Top Forty Under 40 in 2012 for my work on the S.T.OP. Program.

Outside of my work as a law enforcement officer, I've had the luxury of working with the team at Vistelar. They have helped me grow both personally and professionally. My passion is educating people about what police do and why we do it so that the first encounter they have with police can be easy rather than difficult.

As a student, there is a high probability at some point you will have police contact. That is very important to understand. Just because you are stopped by the police doesn't mean that you did anything wrong. That's right. Think about it for a second. If a police officer approaches you and begins asking questions, what is the first thing you think? How do you feel? Scared? Nervous? Anxious? Angry? Confused? Do you immediately think you did something wrong? Do you think that something is wrong?

All of those are great examples of what students have told me about what they're feeling when stopped by a police officer. And it's perfectly normal. Heck, when I'm driving in my personal car and a police car pulls behind me, even I begin to get nervous. What did I do? Are my lights out? Am I speeding? And I'm a cop!! I can only imagine what a citizen would be thinking at this point.

In my program created with Vistelar, "Moment of Truth," we talk about this. We ask students the question, "You've just been stopped by the police. Why did it happen? What do you do?" By utilizing the skills you've learned in this book from Jill, your encounters with police officers will become more positive.

Every city, town or municipality has their own rules. They are called city ordinances. College campuses have their own rules as well. In the story I told in the beginning of the chapter, one of the rules on campus was that students under the age of 21 were not allowed to possess alcohol. Due to my experience, training, time of night, location, the behavior of the students and the fact that all of them illegally crossed the street (jay walking) I chose to stop them and investigate further. City ordinances or rules are created for public safety. These are situations in which police officers have the discretion to stop you and educate you as to what you're doing wrong and how you can improve your behavior.

You might be asking, "Illegally crossing the street? You mean we can't cross the street in front of cars when we have the DON'T WALK signal?" Actually, that constitutes jay walking and you can be stopped by a police officer and questioned. "You mean that I can't carry a red solo cup and walk down the street at night?" Sure, you can carry the cup, however keep in mind that your behavior, time of night, location, speech, smell of intoxicants all play a factor in determining whether you can be stopped by a police officer.

In the program, "Moment of Truth" we also discuss how suspect descriptions play a role in police encounters. I describe the process and there is a neat interactive game that allows students to learn how difficult it is being a police officer and knowing when or when not to stop a person. And don't forget, cops can walk up to you and have a casual conversation at any time. But, just because an officer stops you or stops and talks with you it doesn't mean you did anything wrong. What do you do?

By now you have mastered Vistelar's conflict management skills, right? Vistelar provides you with a template to overcoming any difficult situation – not just an encounter with a police officer. This time-tested program has been used for over 30 years in law enforcement. The skills are effective and necessary for a productive encounter. I've been able to use Vistelar's conflict management tactics in law enforcement, as a youth coach and as a parent. They are powerful skills and a great addition to anyone's tool belt.

If you're stopped by the police, what happens next? Let's talk about your emotions. How are you feeling? Scared? Nervous? Anxious? What happens when you get these feelings? Do you begin to zone out and not hear what the person is saying because you're too scared or nervous? There are five Vistelar tactics you can use to help you effectively manage any difficult situation:

• Showtime Mindset

• Beyond Active Listening

• Universal Greeting

• Redirection

• Showing Respect

The first thing you need to do is to breathe.

In the "Moment of Truth" program we discuss having a "Showtime Mindset." This tactic helps you prepare for the moment. Have you ever given a speech in front of a large crowd? How nervous were you? At some point, you knew that you had to give that speech. You knew you were nervous. While you were getting ready you probably said to yourself, "It's Showtime!" When you see that officer approaching, you should say the same thing. You know something is about to happen so begin to plan for "Showtime" and understand what your next step will be.

Second, you should immediately begin to listen to the officer. I talk about this in great detail in the "Moment of Truth" program. At some point the officer is going to ask you a question, so you should be prepared to answer because you know it's coming.

Listening is more than just hearing words come out of someone's mouth. Listening involves empathy. If you truly understand where the other person is coming from then that encounter will be much more productive. This is what the "Moment of Truth" program provides to the student. This program shows the student the difficulty of being a police officer and in having to make initial contacts. It shows the student how quickly an encounter can turn bad if handled poorly, how quickly it can turn positive if handled well, and the importance of Empathy in having things go well.. Empathy is defined as the ability to understand and share the feelings of others. Put yourself in the officers' shoes. How much difficulty would you have going up to a complete stranger and beginning a conversation, especially if you have reason to believe that this person or someone near or around him has committed or is about to commit a crime?

Show some empathy during your encounter and I guarantee that it will change the outcome to a more positive interaction.

The third tactic you should use when interacting with a police officer is Vistelar's Universal Greeting:

1. Appropriate greeting
2. Name and affiliation

3.   Reason for contact

4.   Relevant question

Police use this tactic all the time.

Step 1   "Good evening."

Step 2   "I'm Officer Smith with the Acme
             Police Department."

Step 3   "The reason why I stopped you is because I got a
             report of loitering on this corner."

Step 4   "Is there any justifiable reason why you're on this
             corner right now?"

This is the Universal Greeting and it is vitally important to the initial contact between police and the community. This template provides the officer with a starting point on how to begin a conversation with a complete stranger. In the "Moment of Truth" program we talked about each of the four steps of the Universal Greeting in great detail and explain the power behind each step. This tactic has helped me tremendously in my 17 years as a law enforcement officer. I've never been in a fist fight with a suspect and I've never had to use pepper spray or my baton on a suspect. I attribute that to the Vistelar conflict management tactics I've learned. I'm a defense and arrest tactics instructor and I understand threat assessment. But I also understand that it is a lot easier to deal with someone when you're not getting punched by them. I'm proud of my ability to communicate effectively with an individual and I believe this ability is one of the most important of the tools I have to manage conflict.

Now that you understand why police use this skill, what if citizens used it as well? Imagine you get stopped by the police. You know at step 4 of the officer's Universal Greeting, he or she is going to ask you a question. What if at that moment you were able to flip the script and use the Universal Greeting on the officer.

Step 1   "Hello Officer."

Step 2   "My name is Tim Johnson."

Step 3   "The reason I'm standing on this corner is
             because I'm waiting for a ride and he's late."

Step 4   "My identification is in my wallet. Would you
             like for me to get it for you? Is there anything
             else you need from me?"

Can you imagine the look on the officer's face if you were to answer his question with this sequence? Everything the officer needs to know will have been answered in a short time frame because you kept your cool, you listened and you answered by using the Universal Greeting. That stop is guaranteed to be more positive because of it.

The fourth tactic you will need when interacting with a police officer is the Redirections tactic. This too is a very powerful tool. Redirections comes in many forms; here are three:

• Funny

• Apologetic

• Serious

Redirections are not always needed, but are very powerful if practiced and then used properly. For instance, if an officer approaches you and asks, "What are you doing standing here on the corner?," you might be feeling a little nervous and want to try to lighten the mood or make conversation by saying:

"I'm sorry officer. I was standing on the corner because I was waiting for a ride. Is there anything I can assist you with?" (apologetic Redirection)

- or -

"Hello Officer. I can tell that something is wrong. I was standing here because I was waiting for a ride. If that is a problem, I can easily wait somewhere else." (serious Redirection)

In the "Moment of Truth" program, we discuss a variety of Redirections that can be used in everyday life and we emphasize the importance of being prepared.. Practice them so they sound conversational. Redirections are a great tool for getting out of difficult situations.

The fifth tactic you will need when interacting with a police officer are Vistelar's five approaches for showing people respect.:

- See the world through their eyes

- "Listen" with all of your senses

- Ask and explain why

- Offer options, let them choose

- Give opportunity to reconsider

If you always try to treat people with dignity by showing respect, I'm confident the majority of your interactions will be positive. By showing respect and having empathy, you immerse yourself into the situation and demonstrate a good understanding of both sides of the interaction. By preparing what you are going to say and when you should say it, your interactions are sure to be more effective.

This chapter provides you with a brief overview on how to deal with police encounters. I provided you with insight as to how police think and talk, tactics you can use when interacting with a police officer. And ways to handle difficult police officers.

I'd like to thank Jill for allowing me the opportunity to be a guest in her great book.

"One of the downfalls of crime prevention training is that you will never know exactly how many crimes you've prevented."

Afterward

Throughout the course of this book, you have learned that you play a crucial role in creating a safe campus environment—one that you will be proud to be a part of and one that you will feel physically and emotionally safe in. It is my sincere hope that you enjoyed the book, but more importantly, that you learned some of the life skills necessary to keep yourself safe on campus and beyond it.

Try to learn as much safety information as you can about your campus before you get there, and during your college career seek out additional opportunities for bystander intervention training and self-defense classes. The more skills that you have to keep yourself safe, the safer you, your friends, and your family will be. Imagine how different the college campus culture could be if all of your friends and family had this type of knowledge and sought out this type of training!

If safety and self-defense training is something that you really enjoy doing, seek out your campus security or police and see if the school sponsors any clubs or activities to help students build personal safety and awareness skills. If they don't, consider getting involved and starting one yourself. You may be surprised at how many like-minded students are out there who are looking to get involved. If you're part of school organization and looking to sponsor a speaker for a special event, such as Spring Break Safety week or Sexual Violence Awareness week, please contact us. We have many professional speaker options, myself included, who can come to your campus and facilitate highly engaging scenario-based training that would benefit students, faculty, staff, and administrators. You can contact us at: info@vistelar.com.

General Personal Awareness and Safety Tips

General Safety Tips

- Always be aware of your surroundings. This includes realizing that you live in a "360 degree environment." You should be constantly looking around. Be especially aware of your surroundings at times when you may be more vulnerable to an attack, such as when walking alone, when you have your headphones on, or if you've been drinking.

- Use discretion when taking "shortcuts" through isolated parts of the campus. Shorter doesn't mean safer!

- Know the location of campus emergency (blue light) phones on routes to and from various campus destinations.

- Keep your personal belongings in view while studying on campus. Never leave your personal belongings unsecured and unattended, not even for "just a few minutes."

- Use the campus transportation services.

When "Going Out" or Walking Alone

- Walk with a purpose. Walk assertively, with a confident posture, and directly to your destination.

- Wear practical footwear. Flip flops, boots, high heels, tight skirts, and baggy pants are hard to run or defend yourself in, and scarves, long necklaces, and chains are easy to grab.

- If possible, modify your fashion style or wear practical, unrestrictive clothing that allows for mobility when walking alone. You can always change into dress-up clothes later.

- Make eye contact with people that are approaching or passing you. We all have an instinct to look away from other people, but looking at the face of potential attackers is a better option as it may scare them off for fear you will be able to identify them.

- If you see people loitering, avoid walking across their path.

- Take off your headphones and put away your cell phone. By keeping your ears open and your hands free, you will be more alert to what is going on around you, rather than with just what's in front of you. This also prevents you from displaying your personal property. This will not only make you safer, but makes you a more aware bystander if someone else needs help.

When Out at a Bar or Club

- Hang out with people you know.

- If you notice someone hanging out or watching your group, ask a friend if they know the person.

- Never accept a drink from a stranger.

- Don't leave your drink unattended.

- Consider splitting your drinks with a friend so to slow down your consumption and not to have to leave it unattended when going to the dance floor.

Walking to Your Car

- Have your keys in your hand as you approach your car so that you don't have to look down or fumble looking for them.

- If you think someone may be following you, walk past your car, or return to the building you left. Don't go to your vehicle.

- Lock your doors when driving and after parking.

- Keep your valuables out of sight, under the seat, or in the glove compartment or trunk.

- Park in well-lighted areas, and if possible, close to the entrance of the building you are going to.

When Taking the Bus

- Sit close to the driver.

- Don't fall asleep.

- Know your route and transfers prior to boarding.

- Know when they stop running.

In An Elevator

- Check the inside of the elevator before entering. Wait for the next elevator if you are unsure of the people inside.

- When riding an elevator, stand by the control board. If you feel in danger, press all the buttons and get off the elevator as soon as possible.

- All elevators are equipped with emergency telephones. Use them if you need to.

Your Residence Hall or Dorm Room

- Your residence hall is your home. Take a share of the responsibility to keep your home safe. We can all make a difference in campus safety, and we all should.

- Keep your room locked — even if you are going to be gone only a "few minutes." Know who is at your door before opening it. Use the "peep" hole in your door.

- Notify campus security/police immediately of suspicious individuals who appear to be "hanging around." Trust your instincts, if someone "appears out of the ordinary," it's safer to call them than "wish you would've."

References

The National Institute on Alcohol Abuse and Alcoholism:
http://www.niaaa.nih.gov/publications

Department of Homeland Security publication:
"How to respond in the event of an active shooter" (2008)

The University of Arizona Step UP! Program:
http://stepupprogram.org/

The Marquette University T.A.K.E.S. A.C.T.I.O.N. Bystander
Intervention Program:
http://www.marquette.edu/dsa/bit/overview.shtml

The Men Can Stop Rape Program:
http://www.mencanstoprape.org/

Acknowledgements

I would like to express my sincere thanks and gratitude to all of the people who helped make this book possible. To Allen Oelschlaeger, Kati Tillema, and Colin Hahn, thank you for your vision and guidance. Without you, this project may never have been completed. To all of the Vistelar Consultants and Advisors who contributed content, thank you for all you do to make this world a better place. You truly are the best in the business, and I am honored to work with all of you.

To my parents, my brother, close family, and loyal friends, thank you for your support. Because of your endless encouragement and confidence in me, I have been able to pursue my dreams. To the Marquette University Police Department, thank you for your unwavering dedication to student safety, and for giving me the tools I need to succeed.

Finally, to the Marquette University Bystander Intervention Team, thank you for your creativity and passion. You are an inspiration to me and I learn from you on a daily basis. The world is safer by the work you do.

About the Author

Jill Weisensel is a consultant and instructor for Vistelar and has campus law enforcement experience, working in part, directing and managing shift patrol operations within an urban campus environment. She is a Defensive and Arrest Tactics Instructor and a Tactical Communication instructor, has taught applications of Tactical Strength and Conditioning at Marquette University, and has a decade of experience in the field. She is also a member of the International Law Enforcement Educators and Trainers Association (ILEETA), the International Association of Campus Law Enforcement Administrators (IACLEA), and the FBI Law Enforcement Executive Development Association (LEEDA).

In understanding the need for non-escalatory tactics and a more effective and professional way to relate with and manage people, she became an advocate of Vistelar's universally applicable conflict management program, and completely integrated it into her Bystander Mobilization training.

Her academic background (Master's degree in Kinesiology with an emphasis in Sports Psychology from the University of Wisconsin-Milwaukee, and Bachelor's degree in Criminal Justice and Sociology from Carthage College), athletic training and professional experience make her uniquely qualified to train and speak on topics such as: the need for personal credibility and professional development, personal safety and self-defense, and the development of leadership and life skills.

Jill has presented her work at multiple Midwest colleges and Milwaukee area events, the 2015 IACLEA National Conference, the 2015 International Association of Chiefs of Police International Conference, the 2016 Virginia Department of Criminal Justice Services Campus Safety Violence Prevention Forum, and the 2017 IACLEA National Conference.

Can You Please Write A Review?

Thank you so much for reading my book! I really value your feedback so it would be wonderful if you could find the time to write a review on Amazon.

When you do this, please send me an email with the "By" name and date of your review so I can check out what you wrote and provide you with a free gift in return for your help.

Please send your email to: reviews@vistelar.com.

I'd Love To Hear Your Peace Story

Now that you've learned how to keep safe on campus, hopefully you've been able to use the skills you've learned.
If so, I'd love to hear your story.

To submit a story, please visit:
www.ConfidenceInConflict.com/peacestories

More Publications From Vistelar

Now that you have an understanding of what Confidence in Conflict means for campus life, please check out our other books in this series: **Confidence in Conflict For ...**

- Everyday Life
- Health Care Professionals
- Sports Officials

Check out our many training manuals: **Conflict Management For ...**

- Everyday Life
- Campus Public Safety
- Law Enforcement
- Private and In-House Security
- Hospitals and Clinics
- Behavioral Health
- K-12 Schools
- Retail Loss Prevention & Security
- Public Utilities

All of these books and manuals are available on Amazon or can be purchased directly from Vistelar.

Members of Vistelar's team come from a wide range of professions and walks of life and, as a result, we have the ability to synthesize our conflict management methodologies with what happens in real life across many work and social environments. Therefore, please watch for other books and manuals in our *Confidence In Conflict* and *Conflict Management* series.

Learning Opportunities From Vistelar

Speaking
In-Person Training
Online Learning

Vistelar is a consulting and training institute focused on addressing the entire spectrum of human conflict at the point of impact — from before an interaction begins through to the consequences of how an interaction is managed. This includes non-escalation, de-escalation, crisis intervention and physical alternatives (e.g., personal protection, defensive tactics).

Vistelar clients include all organizations where human conflict has a high prevalence, such as law enforcement, health care, loss prevention, security, education, customer service and business. In addition the company provides training programs for everyday life (e.g., college students, sports officials, domestic violence).

Vistelar offers a wide range of training programs that address how to:

• Provide better customer service

• Predict, prevent and mitigate conflict

• Avert verbal and physical attacks

• De-escalate conflict

• Control crisis and aggression

• Handle physical violence

The results at the organizational level are:

• Higher levels of customer satisfaction

• Improved team performance, morale and safety

- Reduced complaints, liabilities and injuries
- Protected reputation, culture and business continuity
- Reduced harm from emotional and physical violence
- Decreased stress levels, lateral violence and bullying
- Less compassion fatigue, absenteeism and turnover
- Not having a damaging video show up on YouTube or the evening news

Vistelar's training is focused on the point of impact — the short period of time when disagreements, insults or gateway behaviors, such as swearing or aggressive posturing, can escalate to conflict and on to emotional and/or physical violence.

Vistelar trains "contact professionals" who directly interact with the general public or an organization's clients, as well as organizational teams and individuals who want to improve their performance and life quality by better managing conflict.

Vistelar's methodologies have been proven in real-world environments for over thirty years and are the subject of several books and training manuals in Vistelar's *Confidence In Conflict* and *Conflict Management* series.

Training is provided via speaking engagements, workshops, and instructor schools — using both live and online methods of instruction. Vistelar also hosts its *Beyond Conflict Conference* where attendees have the opportunity to learn the latest about how to effectively manage conflict.

Vistelar's vision is to make the world safer by teaching everyone how to treat each other with dignity by showing respect – via its continued efforts to be the world leader in point-of-impact conflict management training.

To learn more:
Call: 877-690-8230
Email: info@vistelar.com
Visit: www.vistelar.com

Get Immediate Access To a Free Gift

As a thank you for purchasing and reading this book, Vistelar would like to provide you with a **free gift.**

Just go to the URL below to get immediate access.

www.ConfidenceInConflict.com/freegift

Here you can also:

- Access our Training Calendar with registration information for upcoming in-person training programs

- Access our listing of Online Training programs

- Learn about booking a Vistelar speaker at your next event

- Get information about contracting with Vistelar to provide a customized training program for your agency, company, organization or group

- Find out how to host a Vistelar training program at your facility and receive free slots in the hosted class

- Access our online shopping cart with Vistelar books, manuals, online courses, workbooks, apparel and other products

Made in the USA
Middletown, DE
05 May 2018